Better Times Than This

Better Times Than This

Youth Homelessness in Britain

Tom Hall

Pluto Press

LONDON • STERLING, VIRGINIA

First published 2003 by Pluto Press
345 Archway Road, London N6 5AA
and 22883 Quicksilver Drive,
Sterling, VA 20166–2012, USA

www.plutobooks.com

British Library Cataloguing in Publication Data
A catalogue record for this book is available from the British Library

ISBN 0 7453 1624 7 hardback
ISBN 0 7453 1623 9 paperback

Library of Congress Cataloging in Publication Data
applied for

10   9   8   7   6   5   4   3   2   1

Designed and produced for Pluto Press by
Chase Publishing Services, Fortescue, Sidmouth England
Typeset from disk by Stanford DTP Services, Towcester, England
Printed and bound in the European Union by
Antony Rowe, Chippenham and Eastbourne, England

To my mother and father

Difficult to say what all of this is all about.
Being young.

John Ash, 'Poor Boy: Portrait of a Painting'

Contents

Acknowledgements

My first thanks are due to the assorted young people I met on Lime Street and in the bedsit properties nearby, whose lives and difficulties are the focus of this book; and also to the dedicated team of workers at the Lime Street hostel.

The research on which this book reports was supported by a number of institutions. I acknowledge with thanks the financial assistance of the following: Wolfson College, Cambridge; the Ling Roth Fund for anthropological research; the Royal Anthropological Institute, from whom I received a Radcliffe-Brown/ Sutasoma Award in 1995.

Leo Howe has been a fine teacher and a good friend to me for over a decade now; Keith Hart is another friend and mentor (and sometime landlord). Each has a claim to the book's strengths, such as they are.

Terry Roopnaraine and Heather Montgomery were there at the start and watched this work take shape, in an earlier form, with the good humour and understanding that comes from shared endeavour. New friends and colleagues at Cardiff have helped in many ways. I am particularly grateful to Amanda Coffey for taking the time to read through a final draft of this book.

I am also grateful to Anne Beech and all at Pluto Press for their guidance, patience and encouragement.

Penultimate thanks to George Everest for lending me the keys to his flat, where the first few pages of this book were written.

I owe a special debt to Sarah, my beloved wife.

1
Introduction

Leaving central London by train, a journey of a little over half an hour brings you to the town of Southerton. From the train station in Southerton it is no more than a couple of minutes' walk to Lime Street, and halfway down Lime Street is a hostel providing emergency accommodation to the young homeless. I made this journey in 1993, having spent several weeks in the capital city's resettlement units.[1] However, very few of the young homeless who come to stay at the Lime Street hostel arrive, by train or otherwise, from central London. Nor do many travel in the opposite direction, leaving Southerton and making for the hostels, night shelters and streets of the capital (although some do). Youth homelessness in Southerton is a local problem; those using the emergency accommodation that the Lime Street hostel offers are, by and large, local young people – they are homeless at home, in their home town.

Southerton has a population of just under 50,000 people; the town is part of a larger and expanding conurbation lying outside the M25. It is a busily provincial place. The town centre is smallish: a pedestrian high street walled by banks, building societies, department and chain stores and fast-food franchises; and, adjacent to this, an indoor shopping centre with the usual combination of concourse, escalators and balconies. A multi-storey car park, various commercial offices and public buildings – magistrates courts, housing and social services departments – and a municipal park with bright flowers arranged in orderly beds: these complete the picture. Leaving the town centre on foot, shopfronts soon give way to houses and gardens; ten minutes' walk brings you to residential streets, corner shops and muddy playing fields.

The Lime Street hostel, a large, converted, terraced house, stands at just that point where the commercial streets end and the residential ones begin. The properties to either side of the

---

1. The old 'spikes' of George Orwell's time down and out in London.

1

hostel and across the road, like most this close to the noise and traffic of the town centre, are houses of multiple occupancy. There are properties like this in every town and city in Britain, divided into as many single bedsitter rooms as is practicable, each room let out separately to tenants at the bottom end of the private housing market. The houses on Lime Street are typical, if a little shabby-looking, some of them. Ill-fitting curtains are pulled across grimy windows; doorbells with obsolete or indecipherable name tags give little or no clue as to who is in residence. As elsewhere throughout Britain, young people make up a significant number of the total occupancy of these rooms. Many of those who come to stay at the Lime Street hostel are already familiar with rented bedsit accommodation, and the majority of residents eventually move on from the hostel to bedsit rooms nearby, sometimes on Lime Street itself. There is rarely any alternative. A number of these properties must count among the worst maintained in the local private rented sector; the turnover of tenants is high, as invariably evidenced by the piles of 'undelivered' mail in manila envelopes stacked by the skirting boards inside the front doors.

The Young Homeless

When I first arrived in Southerton, Britain was in the grip of a considerable anxiety about its young people. The rise in the incidence of youth homelessness was a particular cause for concern. For those ready to entertain the idea that Britain was host to a burgeoning underclass, the presence of teenagers begging a living and sleeping rough on city-centre streets seemed persuasive evidence – a sign of the times. And as the decade progressed it became apparent that the young homeless numbered many more than those to be seen on the streets of London and a handful of other cities; that, in a less stark and spectacular form perhaps, youth homelessness went much wider and deeper than this; that an unofficial or 'hidden' homeless population numbered

> not only the 2,000 or 3,000 who sleep rough on the streets of London, nor even the 5,000 others who join them on most nights on the pavements of Exeter, Oxford, Brighton, Leicester

and almost any other provincial city ... [but] also the 50,000 mostly young people who are living in squats; the 11,000 in bed-and-breakfast rooms; the 10,000 in hostels for the homeless; the hundreds of thousands cramped on sitting-room sofas and on the floors of friends. (Davies, 1998: 239)

The count dips and spirals. Pat Carlen opens her account of youth homelessness with the assertion that there are over 150,000 young, single adults homeless in Britain (1996: 1); the National Inquiry into Preventing Youth Homelessness puts the figure at 246,000, about one in every thirty young people in the UK between the ages of 16 and 25 (see Evans, 1996: 24). Policy Action Team 12 of the Social Exclusion Unit prefers to cite a source from 1993, which puts the figures at 32,000 homeless 16–21-year-olds in Britain (see Social Exclusion Unit, 2000).[2] Whatever the headline figure, no one doubts that there is a problem, that the numbers are large – alarmingly so – and that youth homelessness in Britain has increased substantially since the 1970s. The background reasons why are well-established. Young people's position in the British housing market, never a particularly strong one,[3] has further weakened as competition for rented accommodation has intensified over the last twenty-five years or so. A general erosion of young people's economic position over much the same period of time, and the contraction of benefit support for the young unemployed, has made things harder still; and for some more than others. Those worst affected by the economic and occupational restructuring, and successive recessions, of the 1980s and 1990s were those poorly qualified school-leavers who could previously have been expected to move directly from school into unskilled, manual work, switching

2. Estimates as to the size of the 'hidden' homeless population are only ever that, and they vary widely. Hutson and Liddiard conclude that the figures available 'tell us very little about the actual problem of homelessness and much more about the organisation collecting them and how it defines homelessness' (1994: 33).

3. Like others disbarred from owner occupation by the high entry costs, young people generally rely on rented accommodation to meet their housing needs; and with no significant access to council housing, it is the private rented sector, in particular, to which most young people turn. Within this sector, they tend to be over-represented as bedsit tenants in houses of multiple occupancy, where conditions are frequently at their poorest and tenure at its least secure (Thornton, 1990: 14).

between a succession of such jobs if they so desired, the compensation for lack of long-term prospects being good money at a young age (Roberts, 1993: 239). Without either prospects or 'good money', some of these young home-leavers have since found themselves struggling to gain any first foothold in the housing market.

Why leave home at all under such unfavourable conditions; why not wait? Why not go back home, if and when (and as soon as) things don't work out? This has been the preference of successive governments; that young people not in work or education, and unable to support themselves financially, be warehoused on training schemes and kept at home – anywhere but on the streets.

Doubtless many young people have done just that; delayed, marked time at home. But leaving home is not something that they can be expected to set aside indefinitely. Patterns of leaving home in Britain have varied over time and according to social background and gender, but doing so – leaving home – has consistently featured as a central element of most young people's move into adulthood, and as such it has a head of normative steam behind it (see Morrow and Richards, 1996: 56). And almost any young person can leave home, even if, and sometimes because, they can do little else; they know where the door is. Added to which 'there are clearly situations where young people leave home because they have to rather than because they want to' (Jones and Wallace, 1992: 108).

Leaving home has become a difficult move, then. Not difficult to do, but difficult to do right; difficult because of the conditions young people face when they leave, and especially difficult for those leaving in a hurry, at a bad time and without much of an option of going back or asking for help.

Us and Them

Homelessness is nothing new of course. There has always been a substantial minority of the population that has struggled to compete effectively in the housing market (Greve, 1991: 4). And young people have always been among these, and have as such figured consistently, perhaps disproportionately, in public anxieties about indigence and the urban poor. Consider, for example, the prominence of children and adolescents – 'street urchins' or the young homeless – in the written and photographic records of nineteenth-century urban destitution (see Hebdige, 1988: 20). Which is not to say that homelessness today is the same as it was a hundred or so years ago. The young people coming to stay at the Lime Street hostel in Southerton are not the 'street-arabs' of Victorian London, in jeans and trainers. But there are continuities. Certainly so in the ways in which (youth) homelessness, now as then, has been woven into wider public anxieties about the 'undeserving' poor.

> Under the Poor Law Acts, passed through the 19th century, paupers or the unsettled poor were put to work in the workhouses. Most were seen as responsible for their position in so far as their poverty was seen to arise from their idleness and fecklessness ... In the 1990s, homelessness is not associated with the housing needs of the majority but with a minority who are still seen as idle and feckless. Public attitudes towards these people today echo earlier sentiments. (Hutson, 1999: 2)

Moral judgement as to the (bad) character of those at the bottom of the social pile has always informed public debate about poverty and the poor; it does so at the present time, just as it did in the Victorian era. The most recent *succès de scandale* in this longstanding debate has been that enjoyed by the American social scientist Charles Murray, whose essays on the emerging British underclass (see Murray 1990; 1994) provoked some comment throughout the 1990s, generating considerable heat if rather less light. In the first of these essays, Murray makes it clear from the outset that he is writing about a poverty that has less to do with low incomes than it has to do with behaviour. His position is unequivocal: 'the "underclass" does not refer to degree of poverty, but to a type of poverty' (1990: 1); its members choose to live as they do, either this or they know no better. If it is the supposedly disaffected young who have provided the sub-text to much of the British underclass debate over the last decade (see MacDonald, 1997: 18), then the young homeless have loomed larger here than most: our most vivid reminder of social exclusion, and exemplars too of the feckless, wilful poor – idle, irresponsible and up to no good; at home (comfortable, that is) at the margins.

Consider Yourself: At Home

This book, an account of youth homelessness, is a work of ethnography; a product of fieldwork.[4] As it happens, I set about fieldwork as a student in a department of social anthropology. It may be that fieldwork and ethnography – as process and product (see Agar, 1996: 53) – are constitutive of anthropology in a way that is not as true for other disciplines (see Wade, 1997: 10), but I do not intend to be jealous about this. I am writing and teaching now as a sociology lecturer in a school of social sciences, and I am happy to have this study fall anywhere within, or outside of, the academic division of labour.

As it happened, I was the only one in my cohort of students not to get on a plane in order to do fieldwork, and in this sense I did my anthropology, my ethnography, at home. Yet fieldwork begins (ought to, ordinarily) with the unfamiliar. The ethnographer, away from home, tries to work through and past this unfamiliarity towards an eventual understanding; towards a point at which he or she is 'at home' in a given research setting perhaps. What then for the ethnographer who has not left home to begin with? The answer, of course, is that there are more ways than one to leave home, and one does not have to pack a passport to do so.[5] Ethnographic exploration on the social margins – the other side of the tracks, not the other side of the world – has a history as long as that of anthropological fieldwork, and the two projects share some of the same strengths and frailties. Each has been informed by a powerful democratic impulse: to take seriously the lives of others. Each has struggled with the tensions and awkwardness, the implicit hierarchies, that come with representation.

The golden age of social exploration – ethnography at home – was the nineteenth century. But, as a mode of inquiry and a genre of writing – with its own distinctive metaphors and

4. I stand by these terms as defined respectively by Maurice Freedman and Anna Grimshaw in *The Fontana Dictionary of Modern Thought* (Bullock *et al.*, 1988).
5. Social anthropology has of course been coming home in a number of different ways for many years now; this move has raised a host of knotty problems and continues to provoke interesting discussion (see Jackson, 1987; Amit, 2000).

concerns – it is very much alive today. *Dark Heart: The Shocking Truth about Hidden Britain* is a work of contemporary social exploration, published in the late 1990s by Nick Davies, a journalist for the *Guardian* newspaper; the book reports on an extended foray into what Davies calls the hidden country of the poor. Borrowing freely from the literary strategies of nineteenth-century social explorers, Davies begins the book with a geographical conceit, as follows.

> I set out to explore this place, pursuing rumours and news reports, and being passed from one contact to another, looking for patterns and themes, trying to record everything I saw like some Victorian explorer penetrating a distant jungle. (Davies, 1998: viii)

The reader is supposed to sit up and take notice. We are about to enter foreign territory, a far away and primitive world that Davies describes as 'utterly different in its way of life' (1998: viii). *Dark Heart* is a sensational and a harrowing book, and Davies is a campaigning journalist concerned that his readers should understand how extraordinarily bad things have got for the poorest of Britain's poor; but these are chancy turns of phrase – a hidden country, a distant jungle, a people whose way of life lies beyond easy comprehension and sets *them* apart from *us*.[6]

In reality (and this is the point, after all) Davies has not had to travel much more than a couple of hours by train to reach any of the places he is writing about. Nevertheless, he insists, these remain hidden territories to the extent that well-meaning people have, for too long, masked the truth about what is happening

---

6. Compare George Sims' *How the Poor Live*, from 1883, which begins as follows: 'In these pages I propose to record the result of a journey into a region which lies at our own doors – into a dark continent that is within easy walking distance of the General Post Office' (Sims, 1976: 65; originally 1883). Or this, from Jack London's *The People of the Abyss*: 'O Thomas Cook & Son, pathfinders and trail-clearers, living sign-posts to all the world, and bestowers of first aid to bewildered travellers – unhesitatingly and instantly, with ease and celerity, could you send me to Darkest Africa or Innermost Thibet, but to the East End of London, barely a stone's throw distant from Ludgate Circus, you know not the way!' (London, 1998: 11, originally 1903). The message is clear: London's East End is further from the civilised society of the day than the very fringes of the Empire; its inhabitants akin to savages (see Kuklick, 1991: 85).

there; have not faced up to the uncomfortable fact that, in various pockets around Britain, poverty has inflicted a deep social damage,[7] which, at its extreme,

> involves the mushrooming of what academics like to call sub-cultures ... little colonies, looking inwards at their own values and rituals, their own ways of surviving. (Davies, 1998: 236)

This is the nub of Davies' argument, and it brings us back to Charles Murray and the dark heart of contemporary underclass fears: the possibility that there are those among the poor who have taken a turn for the worse and can't find their way back, or no longer want to. Murray too insists that this uncomfortable truth has been ducked for too long, if not by well-meaning people then by 'intellectuals'.[8]

Murray and Davies are an unlikely pair; hardly a pair at all. In the final pages of his book Davies dismisses Murray's line of argument as obviously flawed, confusing cause and effect and blaming the poor, where the real culprit is poverty. But Davies has already used this language himself, describing a situation in which 'cause and effect become hopelessly embroiled' (1998: 237). Both writers, either for effect or as part of a wider allegation, portray an exotic world, set apart yet too close to home, where life has settled into some reprehensible, regrettable pattern that will not easily unravel. The implications are far-reaching.

In contrast, the focus of this book is narrow: a few score young people growing up in the same town, most of whom were homeless when I first met them, and many of whom remained intermittently homeless throughout the twelve months that I was in contact with them, moving between episodes of roofless-ness, temporary stays in emergency accommodation and serial residency in a succession of (at best shabby) local bedsit rooms. Nonetheless, the book takes its shape against Davies' scenario –

7. The list of social damage is wide-ranging: crime, drugs, truancy, teenage pregnancy, 'broken families' and also 'a surge in "runaways and throwaways" – children who either fled from their homes or were ejected onto the street' (Davies, 1998: 237).
8. Murray's essay contains a barbed anecdote about a sociology professor who talks with enthusiasm about the 'nice little world that the poor live in', but elects to sit in his car rather than join students on a class exercise canvassing a poor neighbourhood (1990: 17).

little colonies, turned inwards; and it does so questioningly. What is the shape and pattern of life for these young people, homeless off and on and in a host of other difficulties some of them; how are they living, and what, if anything, does this have to do with why they are homeless? These are the questions I hope to answer.

In the Field

What does an ethnographer, a participant observer, do all day? Those engaged in ethnographic research can employ a number of strategies and techniques; for my part I was neither innovative nor exhaustive in my approach. I determined, simply enough, to spend as much time as I could in the company of, and in conversation with, those young people I first met at the Lime Street hostel, keeping a daily written record of things said and done. On arrival in Southerton I rented a small bedsit room five minutes' walk from Lime Street and spent the best part of most days and every evening visiting the hostel. Over time, I was introduced to a wider ambit of young people, and my itinerary expanded to include the high street and shopping centre, the Department of Social Security (DSS) office and the bedsits of those who had moved on from the hostel. Eventually my own room became a venue for residents and ex-residents alike, some of whom even stayed there overnight when they had nowhere else to go.

I had no carefully worked out itinerary for the weeks and months as they passed. My movements on any given day were, by and large, determined by those I happened to be with or bump into. I was probably more sociable than most, trying to make and maintain a wide circle of contacts, and keep in touch with as many of those passing through the hostel, as I could.[9] But even so, my daily round – calling in on friends, meeting up at the hostel, hanging out in the town centre – was little different from that of the majority of those that I was spending time with. Letting the hours unfold in this way, rather than attempting to

9. In all, over the course of a year spent in Southerton I got to know just over a hundred young people, almost all of whom had at some time stayed at the hostel on Lime Street. Some I knew only briefly; others I saw regularly, almost daily, and grew close to.

direct the action or prompt events, made for a fair amount of dull repetition. I passed a good part of each day doing very little – talking about nothing much in cramped bedsit rooms, standing on Lime Street watching passers-by, fidgeting on the fixed seats in the DSS; and although this was often time spent in good company it could be desperately tedious all the same. At other times things got much more exciting and stressful for all concerned, with events racing ahead of my ability to keep track and the young people's ability to cope. My first and lasting impression of those who passed through the Lime Street hostel during the year I spent in Southerton was one of restlessness and inertia combined; time spent with them could be unpredictable and eventful and yet it was somehow always the same.[10]

If repetition is inevitable in the maturation of an anthropologist's understanding, over time, of people's lives, then it is also the case that time, however much one may have of it to begin with, is not forever on the anthropologist's side. And so it can sometimes pay to adopt a more active position, to direct conversations and ask questions; but even here the aim is to do so in as unforced a way as possible. Ulf Hannerz has described how he attempted to strike this careful balance in the course of his own research, and his comments will serve as a summary of the course I tried my best to steer.

> Occasionally I tried to get natural conversations started on topics which interested me particularly. Sometimes these attempts were quite fruitful; at other times they were painfully obvious failures, in which case one could only let conversations proceed to find more spontaneous courses. Of course, I

10. On a more trivial level, another lasting impression I have of fieldwork is of music and cigarette smoke. Each day, it seems to me now, was played out to a soundtrack of chart music, rave or reggae – ticking and fizzing from personal stereos or played loud on a brand new hi-fi, obtained from the mail order catalogue, with little thought as to how to meet the repayments. Cigarettes were also ubiquitous, an essential accompaniment to any activity: something to burn up time with when sitting alone, or to share when you could afford a whole pack; something to 'scrounge' off others when you were broke; something to calm you down after an argument; an accessory on the street, to be held in a certain way and then placed casually in the corner of your mouth or wedged behind the ear, unlit, for later on.

also engaged in direct conversations with people which were consequently somewhat more like interviews, but I tried to give them the form of small talk, and they usually took place in decidedly informal settings, such as on the front staircase of a house ... or over a kitchen table. The results at least usually had 'the ring of truth', that is, they did not seem to constitute an interaction idiom developed specifically for me, and they were generally congruent with what I could observe in other situations. (Hannerz, 1969: 205–6)

The good sense in these observations holds true, despite the important, anxious, reflexive advances that ethnography has since made (see Clifford and Marcus, 1986; Denzin, 1997).

In the first few months of fieldwork I made use of a tape-recorder, sometimes arranging to sit down with individuals and conduct 'unstructured interviews'. Conducting interviews gave me something to do whilst I worked at developing the relationships that I hoped to build my fieldwork around; it also made a certain sort of sense to the residents at the hostel, who were beginning to wonder what I was doing just hanging around all day. But, encouraging as it was to transcribe the tapes and see the sheets of 'data' produced, I was never all that happy with these interviews and eventually stopped doing them altogether. I did not seem to be able to find questions that asked what it was that I really wanted to know; and the answers I got did not always 'ring true'. I was not the only one to feel that these interviews were a little deliberate and forced sometimes.

> *Richie*: Ask Susan to come in, and interview her without her knowing about the tape. And then say to her 'I've taped you and if you want me to I'll wipe it.' It's better that way, innit, cos they react like normal.
> *Craig*: And then pass the tape to me so I can put it on the stereo out loud and really embarrass her.
> *Richie* [to Susan, who has just walked into the room]: He wants to ask you a couple of questions. We've asked each other a couple of questions – about the hostel, about money and that, and, like, where you're going to live after, and jobs and that.
> *Susan* [sarcastic]: Oh, really.
> *Richie* [trying to keep a straight face]: We are, that's what we're doing. Cos he's doing a project thing, or something. Don't look at me like that, I'm being serious.

I also tried to use the tape-recorder in a less formal way, toting it around with me and recording casual discussion of the sort that I was constantly involved in. Here again, I felt that conversations conducted with the tape-recorder on tended to be a little stilted (only subtly so sometimes, but perhaps the more misleadingly for that) or at any rate different from those that I had when the machine was not there to speak into. It may be that I should have set aside my misgivings and persevered. Certainly there are those who have recorded vivid interviews and conversation in the course of ethnographic research (see MacLeod, 1995; Bourgois, 1995; Duneier, 2000); and others (for example, Hecht, 1998) have seen their tape-recorders put to much more creative use than mine ever was. But, as it was, I pretty much stopped using my tape-recorder after the first few months of fieldwork, and was glad to do so. If this book is weaker for that then I am prepared to take some, but not all, of the blame.

Rather than transcripts of recorded conversation, it was fieldnotes that comprised the bulk of the data I took away with me from Southerton, and I have relied on these as my primary source in writing this book. Fieldnotes are hard work. I spent several hours of almost every day in Southerton writing in my notebooks, anxious to get everything down but sometimes fed up with the time it took to do so. I seldom took detailed notes in company, because it proved impractical to do so. I couldn't keep up with events and conversations if I was simultaneously recording these with paper and pen; and even if this had been possible I would have felt uncomfortable doing so, for the same reasons that I felt uncomfortable carrying the tape-recorder around. But I did keep a small notebook with me at all times in which I made (surreptitious) scribbled notes and jottings whenever the opportunity presented. These served as a valuable aide-mémoire when, last thing at night or first thing in the morning, I sat down in my room to write.

Ethics

Fieldwork research with people who are having a hard time of it, whose difficulties and daily frustrations are grist to one's mill, is a morally awkward business. At least I expected it to be. I fretted a good deal about this sort of thing before I got started. Once under way, these anxieties dwindled; I had other things to be getting on with and was glad to have my more abstract anxieties pushed aside by other, more immediate dilemmas.[11] For the most part, I let an everyday and personal ethics inform my relationships in the field, as I would anywhere else.

From the outset I was as open and honest with any young person I met on Lime Street as I felt was right and reasonable, and at least as honest with them as they were with me. Everyone that I got to know at all well, and just about everyone that I met only once or twice, was aware that I was 'doing a project thing, or something' in which they might feature. And just about everyone was happy enough, so far as I could tell, to leave it at that. Every now and then someone would show a passing interest in the notes I was scribbling, but other than this (and demanding – some of them – that their photos appear on the cover of any book I might write) no one was all that interested in what I was up to. I didn't work too hard to overcome this lack of curiosity. I certainly did not feel it was incumbent on me to begin each day and preface each conversation with a reminder that I was a researcher, doing a 'project thing' (which would have been at the very least tiresome for all concerned, if not unworkable in practice). And, of course, as the months went by, it was no longer the case that my research interests exhaustively defined my relationships with the young people whose lives I have described here. I made some good friends in Southerton, for as long as I was there, and over the weeks and months the yardstick against which we measured our relationships with one another had less and less to do with me being a researcher and them being homeless.

11. Mostly to do with my growing knowledge of a range of local, petty, criminal activity – shoplifting, vandalism, car-breaking, drug use and dealing, benefit fraud – in which some of the young people passing through the hostel were involved. Knowledge of these activities was something that I came to take a situational and pragmatic stance on. By and large I kept things to myself, and I do not feel I was wrong to do so. It was certainly not the case that the local police, some of whom I got to know well enough, were eager to file reports on each and every incidence of juvenile crime and misbehaviour that I might have brought to their attention – far from it. On a few occasions I was privy to information about more serious offences, but never under circumstances where I was in the position of being the one to decide whether or not the authorities should be told.

Away from the field, back at my desk and working through my fieldnotes, and because these were friends of mine, I have found myself fretting and anxious again. It has been hard, sometimes awkward, to write at a distance and disinterestedly about life on Lime Street, having known and lived it intimately. Joan Didion may be right to suggest that writers – researchers too – are always selling somebody out (1993, Preface). It may be that research geared to the making of policy recommendations is spared some of this embarrassment, but I suspect it is nothing like as simple as that. In any case, this is not that sort of book.

I can recall only one occasion when I was asked, and then indirectly, about the sort of book I might one day write and the sort of writer or researcher I might be. This was on one of a number of evenings when Roy, 16 years old and three months out of local authority care, called in to my bedsit room to pass the time and see if I had any cigarettes. Rifling through my things he picked up some books by my bed and started to quiz me about them: 'What are these books, man?' And then, having listened distractedly to my explanation: 'Anthropology, sociology, what's that?' And then, putting the books aside: 'Oh, I get you. It's like people talking and that. What goes on in a place and people talking about it.' Which seems to me to be a good enough description to be going on with.

No one from Lime Street has their picture on the cover of this book, and although most of the young people that I ever discussed it with were happy enough at the time for their names to be used, I have opted instead for confidentiality. I have changed the names of people and places; I have also shuffled some minor details of biography and circumstance, without, I hope, doing violence to the truths of this account, such as they are.

2
At the Hostel

The young people who come to stay at the hostel on Lime Street are homeless; out of house and home, for whatever reason. Most call at the hostel in the choppy wake of some or other family argument, arriving late at night, angry and upset having just 'walked out', or turning up, bedraggled, after a couple of days spent staying with friends, squatting or sleeping rough. Others have been away from home and living independently for some time but have run into difficulties, lost their accommodation and do not see returning to their parents to be an option. Still others have no family home to speak of.

At 16 years old, and newly arrived at the hostel, Cherie already has an eventful and involved housing history behind her:

Cherie: I was just fed up with the rules and that. My dad was quite strict with me really and I'd just had enough. I didn't get on with them at all when I was at home, so I just, like, up and left. We had a big row and fighting and that first of all ... I stayed at my friend Sue's place up the road for the weekend until I got somewhere sorted. Then I went and stayed with my nan, but I got into a bit of trouble there. I was out till all hours and I started doing drugs and I was always out with boys – different boys and that. Then I moved back home. I don't know why. My mum wanted me to, and in a way I did [too], but [at the same time] I didn't [really want to]. So I went back home but we had another big row and my mum said to get the hell out, so I did. But the police picked me up and took me back and they had a word with my mum and she made it clear that she didn't want me back so they put me into emergency accommodation ... in the end I moved in with this guy called Jim. We was really good mates and that, and if I didn't have any money he'd help me out and he was always there, sort of thing. But everything went wrong ... I phoned my social worker but she wouldn't rehouse me cos I'd done so many bunks before, and she said I had to report what had happened to the police, and she said I'd be housed if I did it that way. So I went and got a doctor's report, but those two stuck together and it was just me and my witness, and she wouldn't come forward cos she was only a young girl and she had a little baby and

15

another one on the way. So I had to drop the charges. So I tried a couple of places, but they didn't have no accommodation for me so I come here.

Cherie's story is her own, and perhaps longer than most, but it is not out of place alongside those of the hundred or so other young people who come to stay on Lime Street each year.

First Impressions

The hostel itself stands about half way down Lime Street, a mid-terrace, ordinary-looking residential building – no security cameras or bars on the windows or anything like that, no sign outside even. Only the general traffic in and out of the building (and the level of noise) sets it apart from the properties to either side. In fine weather the hostel spills out into the street: the front door ajar and the pavement outside occupied by residents, friends and hangers-on, standing around, showing off and scattering cigarettes; music thumps out of open windows. All of which can be a little daunting. Even Cherie, who is as cocky and effervescent as they come, took two passes at the hostel before she got up the nerve to cross the street and ring the bell. Things are quieter late at night and over the winter, with doors and windows closed up against the cold; all the same, newcomers stepping up to the front door must still meet the combined scrutiny of residents in the hostel's front room, looking up from the glow of the television.

Inside, standing in the hallway, the front room is to your left. Barely visible through a pall of cigarette smoke, residents are wedged into comfy chairs or sprawled across each other's laps on the sofa, trading gossip, jokes and insults over the noise of the television. Overflowing ashtrays and empty mugs are arrayed on a low table in the middle of the room and scattered across the floor; a niggling discussion drags on as to who should get up to make the next round of coffees.

New arrivals are led past this room on down the hallway to the staff office, a much smaller room into which a large desk, computer workstation, filing cabinet and two office chairs have been squeezed. Above the desk, ex-residents grin and grimace out from a collage of snapshots pinned to the wall: eating breakfast, half asleep; holding a new baby; pushing past one another, in a blur, to get at the camera. Once stacks of paperwork have been cleared away, and with the door firmly closed for privacy, the business of booking in begins: details are taken, forms are filled in, the house rules are explained. Back in the front room a hurried round of speculation and assessment begins: what did he look like; does anybody know her; whose room will he be sharing?

The only other room on the ground floor, at the back of the building, is the kitchen. This large room is usually empty – smoking is forbidden here. At mealtimes, however, the kitchen gets frantic, as dirty pans pile up on the counter and residents crowd round a table big enough to seat only eight. When the hostel is full, this does not suffice and anyone getting up from the table to fetch a glass of water during the meal is likely to find that their seat is occupied when they return. Some residents eat standing up or on the move, ready to go out for the evening. Those who have already finished, or are not hungry, stand outside the back door by the bins, smoking.

Upstairs there are beds for a total of ten residents in four shared bedrooms (and a small storeroom that doubles as a staff bedroom). The girls' room, sleeping two, is usually (not always) the tidiest of these. Magazines and photographs are arranged on bedside tables and the windowsills are lined with small boxes and bottles of perfumes and shampoos; a hamster sleeps in its cage on top of the wardrobe. The boys' rooms (a twin and two triples) smell of socks and trainers; the curtains have worked loose in places and hang crookedly from the rails; supermodels and Bob Marley stare down from the walls at heaps of clothes on the floor. These rooms only get busy at night when the lights are turned off downstairs and protesting residents are ushered up to bed. There is much banging of doors, shouting and charging up and down the corridors at first, but this clamour soon dwindles away (or stops abruptly, if the member of staff on duty decides that he or she has had enough). With the bedroom doors closed and the hostel now quiet, anyone known to have cigarettes is pestered to 'splash' them round for a last smoke.

A Miscellany

The hostel plays host to an inconstant assortment of young people, some of whom stop over for no more than a single night before moving on elsewhere. Most stay longer, a few days at least and perhaps up to eight weeks, which is the maximum residency the hostel offers; and while all must leave eventually, the hostel staff can be sure of seeing some residents again before long. Tony is one of twenty or so young people who have become 'regulars': familiar faces on Lime Street.

> *Tony*: ... [the first time that I stayed at the hostel] they found me a bedsit. I was there for about four and a half weeks and then I got kicked out. The landlord was a bit of a wanker. He kicked all the under-18s out for no reason. So I went back to the hostel. That must have been November. I stayed for about a month and then I found another place, but I didn't like it there either cos I didn't get on with any of the residents. I was 17 when I moved in there. People were always fighting and the landlord wouldn't do nothing about it and I just got jacked off with it. Then I moved back again and the staff found me a place on a training scheme. I was at the hostel two months that time, until just before Easter. Then over Easter I went home cos I was talking to my mum again. But my mum can only stand me for so long, and I can only stand her for so long, so in January I moved back to the hostel.

Many residents remain in touch with the hostel for some time after they have left Lime Street, even if they do not return to stay there. Vicky, one of the hostel's first ever residents, still visits infrequently, whenever she feels like company or has run out of cigarettes, although it is almost a year now since she left the hostel to move into a bedsit of her own. The hostel staff generally encourage this and do their best to support ex-residents, although this can involve them in work beyond the remit of their official duties.

While all the young people coming to stay at the hostel are in immediate and emergency need of accommodation, only a small minority arrive directly from 'the streets'. Bagsy is one of those few residents with any sustained experience of sleeping rough, having at one time joined the ranks of London's street homeless:

> *Bagsy*: I lived on the streets in London and it ain't nice, not nice at all. That was when I was 15 years old ... I was there for about two or three months with my sleeping bag and my kit of clothes. In the end I just phoned up my old man and the old man come up, sorted

me out, dropped me off [in Southerton] and goes 'Right, you're on your own', and I got bunged back in a children's home.[1]

Others who have, like Bagsy, experienced the sharp end of the homeless wedge have generally done so closer to home. Graham was evicted from his bedsit for bringing drugs onto the premises, and slept out in a garden shed for a couple of nights before he found out about the hostel. Marty was enterprising enough to 'walk out' on his dad with a tent on his back, which he set up in the local park for the best part of a week. But most young people coming to the hostel have not (yet) had to sleep rough. Some arrive within hours of leaving home or losing their accommodation, others have managed to string together a succession of nights with friends and relatives before running out of favours. After acrimonious rows with his mum's new boyfriend, Jack was 'kicked out' of home and stayed a couple of nights with his grandparents and then several weeks with his girlfriend at her parents' house before coming to Lime Street. Graham's girlfriend Yvonne left her ex-partner after a violent argument and slept on the sofa in her mum's lodgings for several nights until the live-in landlady asked her to make other arrangements. Some young people arrive at the hostel after months of making do in similar *ad hoc* and stop-gap living arrangements.

One way or another, most young people come to Lime Street following some sort of family row. For a few, conditions at home have clearly been intolerable. But many more call at the hostel following rather ordinary domestic arguments. Vicky left home after a row about the hours she was keeping. Having come home late once too often she got into a shouting match with her parents which ended with her mum dragging her upstairs to her bedroom; later that night, angry and upset, she packed a bag and walked out. Looking back on events, Vicky readily concedes that this was a 'stupid argument', no more dramatic or decisive than any number of other rows she was having at home at that time. Still, she insists that if she had not walked out on this occasion then she would certainly have done so before long, because of

1. At 15 years old Bagsy would have been too young to stay on Lime Street. It is generally an offence to 'harbour' a young person under the age of 16 who has left home; special provision does exist for the setting up of refuges which are exempt from the laws on harbouring, but these are few and far between (see The Children's Society, 1999: 9–13).

some other quarrel. Many young people, like Jack, have 'walked out' following arguments with, or about, a new family member at home. Keith is another of these. He left home claiming that his mum's new boyfriend had been pushing him around and had smashed up his stereo. Keith's mum tells a different story: Keith was argumentative and difficult around the house and unwilling to give her new partner a chance. Al, who has shared a bedroom at the hostel with Keith, had thought he was getting on OK with his mum's boyfriend, and had even been allowed to borrow his car a couple of times. But, having taken the car away for a weekend without asking he returned to find his mother furious, the car reported stolen and his things packed in the hallway. Arguments about money – money borrowed, money owed, money gone missing or taken without asking – are another source of family rifts. For Graham it was mounting tension at home about his unemployment that prompted him to leave to find a place of his own (and mostly pride that prevented him from going back once he lost his bedsit).[2]

Bagsy's experience of homelessness on the streets of London may be uncommon on Lime Street, but his background in local authority care is less so. A steady flow of young people coming to the hostel are care-leavers, and it is close to a majority of residents who have some history of contact with the social services.[3] Social workers regularly contact the hostel looking for accommodation for clients, as do probation officers. The staff at a young people's advice project in the town centre – known locally as the ABC project – phone the hostel almost every day to check on vacancies. Occasional referrals also come in from the network of other hostels and night shelters in the surrounding area. Robert came to Lime Street late one night after a phone call from a (full) shelter in a neighbouring town; by his own account, he has spent over a year moving around between hostels and night shelters all over the south-east of England in a nomadic existence that he has grown accustomed to and almost enjoys. Tim is another from

2. Young men's unemployment seems to generate greater domestic tensions than young women's. This may be explained by enduring social perceptions of employment, which make female unemployment appear less of a problem (see Hutson and Jenkins, 1989: 29).
3. Research consistently shows the young homeless to include disproportionately large numbers of care-leavers (see, for example, Evans, 1996; Strathdee, 1992; Thornton, 1990).

the 'hostel circuit', a young man lacking Robert's savvy and charm, whose mental health problems have made him unpopular with other young people wherever he has stayed. Since leaving home three months ago he has been passed and pushed from one hostel to another, at ever decreasing intervals.

The Lime Street hostel is a direct access project, which means that prospective residents do not need to be referred there by a third party. Young people can, and do, simply turn up at the front door alone and unannounced. As a general rule if a young person calls looking for a place to stay and there is a vacancy then they can move in immediately; residency is restricted only by age – the hostel is open only to young people aged 16 to 25 (although see also page 27). In practice the residents cluster towards the bottom end of this range; most are in their mid to late teens. Some residents are of school age and, of these, a few are still in education despite the disruption caused by their present circumstances. Jack has made it to school most days through nearly a month of stop-gap living arrangements, and continues to do so at the hostel, where he is woken early each morning by the staff. Tara, who was 'kicked out' of home following family arguments and referred to Lime Street by her social worker, is presently suspended from school, but she has GCSE exams coming up and makes sporadic attempts to study for these. Others of the same age are quickly leaving school days behind them. Suzie has not attended school once since 'walking out' of home two months ago and is now making plans for the birth of her baby. The baby's father, Suzie's boyfriend Brian, is in prison on remand.

Richie is another who has spent time in prison. Now in his late teens, he has been out of education, in trouble with the police and intermittently homeless for several years.

Richie: Well, my old man used to send me to school in flares and stuff like that, and he thought that was a good idea, to make me stick up for myself. And I needed to wear glasses and he give me National Health ones, he thought 'Yeah, that'll make him stick up for himself.' But it didn't. What happened, I was getting so much hassle I didn't bother going to school. When I was twelve, I just thought 'Fuck it, I don't want to go to school no more', so I didn't. I didn't go to school, only now and again when I could be bothered. Just bummed around nicking this and that, and stealing ... I done crime since I was about 13. Then I done a runner from home ... we used to have arguments and I'd walk out. And when I was 16 I got kicked out of my house and I was on the streets then for a long time. I used to live on a park bench for a little while, then I lived in a garage for a few weeks, no, a few months actually ... then I went to prison and come out and went inside again.

Richie might seem an altogether different young person from Siobhan, who has never once been in trouble with the police, and left home for the first time only two weeks ago. But today, sat together on the sofa holding hands, they seem an ordinary young couple, and it is anyone's guess as to how their futures will unfold. Things hang in the balance for both of them.

The same could be said of any of the hostel residents; they are a chequered crowd, with doubtless chequered fortunes to face. But for the moment at least they are all in much the same boat. Some might be described as 'problem' young people, from problem backgrounds, but labels of this sort can obscure as much as they reveal. They are all, in their way, quite ordinary young people – local kids, none of them from any kind of privileged background, not all that successful at school, out of work (like plenty of others their age), living away from home and in a jam at the moment, but optimistic where they can afford to be and resilient where they cannot. Few of them would stand out in a crowd, despite the best, and well-intentioned, efforts of the local church congregations that supply the hostel with occasional donations of clothing – cardboard boxes full of knitted cardigans and old suit trousers, which the residents unpack with a mixture of hilarity and dismay, and never wear.

The Staff Team

Like most accommodation projects for the single homeless, the hostel is a voluntary sector initiative. The property was purchased and renovated through the fund-raising efforts of a local charity, Southerton Housing.[4] Ann, the hostel manager, and Kevin, her

---

4. Operational costs, including staff salaries, are met through a combination of housing benefit payments (paid directly to the hostel for each young person in residence), grant money and some local authority funding. Like a great many voluntary sector initiatives, Southerton Housing's finances are precarious, dependent on short-term funding arrangements.

deputy, are employed by Southerton Housing and have worked
at the hostel since it first opened a little over a year ago.
Additional funding has since made it possible to employ a third
worker – Poppy, in post now for two months. Philip, a full-time
volunteer on a six-month placement at the hostel, completes the
staff team. With occasional help from a roster of one-evening-a-
week volunteers, these four are responsible for the daily running
of the hostel, providing support and supervision for residents
during their stay and assisting them in moving on into more
settled accommodation.

The 'mission statement' for the Lime Street hostel, drawn up
by the management committee of Southerton Housing, reads as
follows:

> we see the provision of emergency accommodation as only the
> first step in integrating the young single homeless back into
> the community ... [the hostel] aims to provide a breathing
> space where young people's needs are acknowledged so they
> can consider their options, decide how they want to spend
> their immediate future and make realistic choices ... an oppor-
> tunity for young people to take time to evaluate what has
> happened in their lives and provide them with resources to
> turn it around ... a stable base from which to establish their
> goals and break the cycle of instability and homelessness.

And although staff members might permit themselves a wry
smile at the easy ambition here, they would not dispute the
general intent. Ann, the hostel manager, outlines the goals she
shares with her co-workers in much the same language:

> *Ann*: Our goal for them [the residents] is to help them to leave into
> accommodation – leave properly, and move on to having a more
> stable lifestyle. In order to give them the skills for having a more
> stable lifestyle, while they're at the hostel the agreed goals, for
> example, are that they learn to budget, learn to have a realistic idea
> of their employment, sign on for benefits or training. So, with Becky
> and Jim, all they're interested in is finding a place together ... with
> Marky, we need to be thinking about his drug and alcohol problem
> while he's here.

And Joy, one of the regular volunteers, speaks for all who work
at the hostel when she says that the hostel should be

... more than just a place where they [the residents] come and sleep at night ... I'd like to think I was taking part in something that was trying to achieve more. Maybe it's taking on more than we can handle, but I think [for example] raising self-esteem is something we can all be doing, just building relationships with them and motivating them to take a look at where they are and where they want to go in their life.

The staff can only do so much, of course, and many of the young people coming to Lime Street life face difficult futures. All the same, the expectation is that residents should make the most of what the hostel has to offer them during their stay; should measure up, as best they can, to the difficulties they face and see the sense in doing so. The staff team look to strike a fine balance here. They offer reassurance, understanding and encouragement, and hope thereby to foster responsibility, independence, self-discipline, maturity ...

> Kevin: ... constructiveness and motivation, I think, is vital to them. And if they don't have that coming from us, then eight weeks later they're the same person that came in the door ... I know it's a catch-22 situation with a lot of them [given the difficulties they face] ... yet it's still the motivation [that matters].

So says Kevin, Ann's deputy. Kevin is a charismatic presence around the hostel. Having experienced homelessness (and drug addiction) himself and made a definitive break with that period of his life, he is keen that the young people coming to Lime Street should set about 'making a change' in their own lives. He is generous with his time and sympathy but does not see it as his job to 'babysit' anyone; it annoys him that some residents do not seem to take on board 'what they're taught or being told to do by the staff'. A university graduate, Ann came to Lime Street having worked in a residential project for children with behavioural problems. She and Kevin get along very well, but they differ in their approach to work at the hostel. Where Kevin challenges, Ann prefers to coax. She has more patience for those who

> ... come in [to the office] and want to talk and talk and talk, and not really talk about anything – just go through what's been happening to them.

Poppy is the youngest member of the staff team, young enough to stay as a resident, were she homeless.[5] She is an enthusiastic new recruit, popular with the residents and a softer touch than either Ann or Kevin. On her evenings off, she sometimes calls round to the hostel just to spend time chatting with residents in the front room. Philip, the full-time volunteer, likes to run his shifts with minimal fuss. He does not spend time in the front room and discourages residents from hanging out in the office. Before coming to Lime Street, he worked as an assistant in a cold-weather shelter in central London and he thinks that, on the whole, the residents on Lime Street have 'a pretty easy ride' compared to the older, street homeless population.

Work at the hostel takes its tempo from the chance events of the day and the current mix of people living there. The staff have to respond flexibly to this, and they do so as a team, with good sense and the best intentions: befriending, supervising, counselling and arbitrating between up to ten young people at any one time, seeing them through no more than two months of their lives before starting over again with new faces. The job can be tense and wearing, but also rewarding, and with Ann and Kevin as its mainstay the team has things running on a fairly even keel. They cannot do all that they would like to do for every single resident, but they do enough to feel that they are making a difference – achieving something, some of the time, with some of the young people they work with, and at the very least providing a bed for those with no place of their own to stay.

Signing In, Signing On

In all the time that the hostel has been open the stream of young people coming to Lime Street looking for a place to stay has never once dried up. On any given day there is likely to be the full complement of ten residents on Lime Street; as and when vacancies arise they are filled in a matter of days, sometimes hours.

5. Ann and Philip are not much older than Poppy, both in their late twenties; Kevin is almost 40.

*   *   *

Rhys, 22 years old and homeless, is in the office with Ann; the ABC project has sent him over, knowing there is a vacancy. Rhys has stayed at the hostel once before but did not feel comfortable sharing a room with strangers and left after only one night.[6] Since then he has been making do with stop-gap living arrangements, relying on friends to put him up for a night or two whenever possible; for the last two weeks he has been sleeping rough in a derelict building.

Over a cup of tea and cigarettes, Ann asks Rhys a little about his background. He tells her that he spent most of his childhood in local authority care and has no immediate family in the area; he has been without a permanent address for several months. Ann asks, as she does with all new arrivals, if Rhys uses drugs. He tells her no. She asks if he has a criminal record and Rhys explains that he has previous convictions for petty theft and shoplifting and is due to appear in court on similar charges next week.

Ann gives Rhys an application form for housing benefit (to cover the cost of his rent for up to eight weeks' residency at the hostel), which he fills in with her help. She explains that he will have to pay an additional £2 per day 'kitchen money' if he wants to eat at the hostel. Next she reads through the house rules, which detail the daily schedule at the hostel, the residents' rota for cooking and cleaning, health and safety regulations and prohibitions on theft, violence and the use of drugs and alcohol on the premises.

Rhys signs a copy of the rules and Ann shows him the bedroom he will be sharing and then introduces him to the residents sitting in the front room. Leaving him in there, she returns to the office to file away his paperwork.

'They're now undoing all the things I've just been through with him', she explains, smiling wryly.

*   *   *

This vignette is repeated, with minor variation, every time a young person comes to stay at the hostel. New arrivals sit down in the office with a member of staff, tell their story, answer

---

6. Fear of violence, bullying and intimidation, drug use and theft are among the most common reasons why some young homeless people are reluctant to use hostel accommodation, even when there are places available (see Scanlon, 2001).

questions, fill in forms and sign their name to a copy of the house rules. From start to finish the procedure takes not much more than half an hour, but it is an important half hour. Walking into the office Rhys is homeless, walking out he has a bed for the night and accommodation for the next eight weeks should he want it, an address at which he will be registered for social security and housing benefit and at which his solicitor can contact him. As a resident at the hostel he is pledged to a domestic routine, with hours to keep, rules to abide by, regular meals (to be budgeted and paid for) and a part to play in the daily upkeep of the premises.

The intention to provide the young homeless of Southerton with 'a stable base from which to establish their goals and break the cycle of instability and homelessness' (see page 23) is thus set in train as soon as a new arrival is signed in at the hostel. That is the idea, at least. Things do not always run quite so smoothly, as Ann's closing comment intimates.

Although admission to the hostel routinely operates on a first come, first served basis, there are exceptions. Not every young person who comes to Lime Street looking for a room is offered one. The hostel is not open to young people with criminal convictions for arson or sex offences, or to intravenous drug users (although staff members cannot always know whether or not a new arrival falls into any of these categories, unless such information is volunteered).[7] Staff members are similarly wary of accommodating young people with mental health difficulties and those who present very 'challenging' behaviour. But there is no hard-and-fast rule here, and with only a cursory assessment of eligibility prior to residency – ten minutes' conversation over a cup of tea in the staff office – they usually err on the side of beneficence.

Each new arrival at the hostel is of course different from the next. Some seem more needy and vulnerable than others, some are flippant or unforthcoming about their circumstances, still others are awkward or hostile or grateful or comic. Some, staff members suspect, will be hard work to have around the place –

---

7. The rationale here is not a punitive one: in the absence of special training and facilities, the intention is to protect the health and safety of residents (and volunteers and staff).

those whose 'attitude' is all wrong from the start. But the temptation to exclude or discourage such young people runs up against what the staff see as their first and foremost duty: the provision of accommodation to all comers, even and especially those who may prove difficult to help and rehouse. And so, although questions of suitability (rather than eligibility) may be at stake in the processing of new arrivals,[8] they rarely surface.

Discrimination plays much more of a part when decisions are made as to whether or not to admit a young person already known to the hostel staff. Strangers are welcome; those who have blotted their copybook on previous stays at the hostel (by using drugs on the premises or starting fights with other residents, for example) are not always so, and the staff sometimes choose to exclude them. Such decisions are tricky, and seldom final. When Simon asks Poppy if he can come back to stay only two weeks on from his eviction from the hostel for using drugs on the premises, he is told in no uncertain terms that he will have to look elsewhere; three months later he is in residence again, the staff team having reconsidered and relented.

Sometimes more complex considerations are brought to bear on a decision to admit a new resident.

*   *   *

Robby is 17 years old and left home only a few months ago, having fallen out with his parents; since then he has been sleeping on the sofa at a friend's house. He has been a regular visitor to the hostel for several weeks, stopping by in the evenings to call in on Pete and Roger, whom he first met hanging around the games arcade in the town centre. In the course of these evening visits the staff team have got to know Robby quite well and have taken an interest in his situation; Poppy has been working with the ABC project to try and find him a place of his own. Her efforts are overtaken by events, however, when Robby arrives at the hostel one morning with the news that his temporary living arrangements have miscarried, leaving him homeless. His arrival coincides neatly with Pete's departure – Pete has moved out to a rented room on Springfield Avenue, overlooking the railway

8. Michael Lipsky (1980) has done much to expose and explore the informal processing of clients by what he calls street-level bureaucrats; his analysis is relevant here.

station, and his old bed (in a room shared by Roger) is empty. Philip is on duty and he signs Robby in as a new resident.

When Ann turns up to work the evening shift Robby is waiting for her in the hallway; his bags are already unpacked.

'Hi Ann', says Robby. 'I bet you're pleased to see me.'

'Well, no actually Robby. I mean, I'm pleased to see you, but I'm not too happy that you're here.'

In the office, Ann tells me she is not convinced that Robby will benefit from coming to stay at the hostel. It disturbs her that he seems, if anything, a little pleased to be a resident and no longer just an occasional visitor. This is not the way it should be. She worries too that Roger is a poor influence on him. Had she been on duty when Robby first arrived, she might have tried to dissuade him from moving in, offering him a bed only if he absolutely could not make other arrangements, and then only for a night or two – time in which to patch things up with the friend he had been staying with. She has no problem with Robby coming to stay *per se*, but would rather see him cope on his own as he has done thus far, albeit with difficulty, than have him come to rely on the hostel 'and get into the whole homeless thing'.

* * *

Robby is certainly eligible to stay at the hostel. In many ways he is an eminently suitable resident, just the sort of young person that the staff are there to help. He can be trying and rowdy at times, but is also vulnerable and, in his more sober moments, has talked seriously with members of staff about his future hopes and fears. Yet Ann has misgivings about his coming to stay. Her feeling that the hostel should not be so ready to house Robby reflects a complex concern for Robby's best interests and for the staff team's motivations in the matter.

Almost every young person coming to stay at the hostel is out of work and entitled to state benefits, principally a means-tested income,[9] and assistance in paying rent. Some are already 'signed on' for social security and have little more to do on arrival than complete an application form for housing benefit and register their change of address. Others, especially those who have been on the move and homeless for anything more than a couple of

9. Very few have paid enough national insurance contributions to qualify for contributory benefits.

weeks, arrive with their benefit claims in a state of some disarray. Scott is one such – evicted from the bedsit at which he was last registered for benefit and frustrated in his subsequent attempts to get the DSS to issue him with an over-the-counter payment, he has abandoned his claim as a dead loss. He arrives on Lime Street worn down by three weeks spent with no fixed address and no income. Katy is another who has struggled to stay on top of her benefit entitlements. She arrives at the hostel with a dog-eared file containing 15 letters from the Benefits Agency, running to 40 sides of paper in total – an incomplete record of her benefit entitlement over only the last two months, during which time she has moved house three times. The most recent letter informs her that her claim for benefit, at an address at which she is no longer resident, will be forfeit unless she attends a rescheduled interview, the date for which is now past. Some of the youngest arrivals, those who are just out of school and away from home for the first time, have never claimed benefits before.

And so, one way or another, most new residents spend the best part of their first full day at the hostel sorting out their benefits. This can be a tiresome and convoluted process; especially so for the 16- and 17-year-olds, who must deal with, and trek between, three different offices: the Careers Service, the Employment Service JobCentre and the Benefits Agency or DSS.[10] But getting properly signed on is a priority so far as the staff team is concerned, and is close to being a condition for continued residency at the hostel. The hostel cannot operate without the housing benefit income it receives from the local council for each young person staying there; in addition to which, ensuring that residents are in receipt of, and responsible for, a regular income is a part of the wider agenda to which the staff team are working (as Ann indicates on page 23).

A little over two weeks into her stay at the hostel, Katy's battered file is a little thicker; her housing benefit application has

10.   The Benefits Agency is, or was, an executive agency of the Department of Social Security; the two are not identical. However, staff and residents at the Lime Street hostel always refer to the Benefits Agency as the DSS (I have adopted the same convention throughout much of this book). As of April 2002 an executive agency of the Department for Work and Pensions, called Jobcentre Plus, has replaced both the Benefits Agency and the Employment Service (see Child Poverty Action Group, 2002: 3).

been processed and her fortnightly social security income has been (re)calculated at £61.44. Breakfast and an evening meal at the hostel, and as much tea and coffee as she can drink, will cost her £28 in kitchen money over the next two weeks, leaving her with a daily allowance of £2.39.[11]

Residency

Some residents leave Lime Street long before their benefits catch up with them. A very few, luckier or more resourceful than most, find themselves a room to rent in a matter of days; others decide to patch things up with their parents or the boyfriend they walked out on; still others simply disappear, leaving no forwarding address. But most stay for longer than this and many end up on Lime Street for close to the full eight weeks, glad enough to have a fixed address and in no great hurry to leave any sooner than they have to. As hostels go it is not such a bad place to stay; the building is maintained to a high standard, the facilities are good, and the decor and furnishings are at least on a par with those in the privately rented bedsit rooms in and around Southerton's town centre. Provided that they keep to the house rules and do their share of the cooking and cleaning, residents are pretty much free to spend their time as they choose. Shelley's commentary on her residency is typical.

> *Shelley*: Just doss around all day – that's what I've been doing, until recently. I think that everyone that's here's done that. They've stayed here and then, when they find that, you know, when it's near to the end to when they have to move out, they start looking [for accommodation] then. That's what I've done anyway. When I first moved in I wanted to stay, I couldn't be bothered to look for anywhere [else]. I was just making it my life, and that was it.

Those, like Shelley, who make the hostel their life for a couple of months, settle to a rhythm. Days spent in residence follow a

11. These figures are from 1994, and include deductions – at £5.43 per week – for repayment of a loan from the social fund; Katy would be about £6 a week better off today (see CHAR, 1994; Child Poverty Action Group, 2002). The detailed rules of entitlement, and guidance issued on these, change year on year; the difficulties the young homeless face in securing their benefit entitlement do not; those aged 16 and 17 have things especially hard.

simple timetable. Each new day begins at half past eight in the morning with a member of staff knocking on the bedroom doors to wake those still sleeping. All residents have to be up, out of bed and downstairs by 9 o'clock in time for breakfast, after which there are household chores to be done – the dishes to be cleared away and washed, the kitchen floor to be mopped, the front room to be vacuumed, beds to be made and bins and ashtrays to be emptied. On weekdays the hostel shuts up at 11 o'clock in the morning and residents must find somewhere else to go for the rest of the day. Most – those not at school or college or on a training placement – spend their time either visiting friends or wandering around town, window shopping and doing nothing.[12] The hostel opens up again at 5 o'clock in the afternoon, by which time there is usually a small crowd of bored residents waiting on the pavement outside; dinner is served up an hour later at 6 o'clock or thereabouts. At half past ten the hostel starts to close up for the night – the kitchen is cleaned and locked up, the lights are turned off downstairs, the burglar alarm is set; by half past eleven everyone is (supposed to be) upstairs and in bed.

*   *   *

It is half past ten on a Friday morning. Richie, Paula, Tony, Graham and Roy are sitting on the sofa in the front room waiting for Craig to finish vacuuming and plug the television back in. Three residents have already left the house: Chris and Siobhan have gone to school, under protest, and Terry has cycled off to work a shift in the kitchen at a local fast-food restaurant.

Kevin pops his head round the door to remind those remaining that the hostel is closing. Richie, Craig and Graham have no particular plans for the day. They will head into town and wander around window shopping for a while, and then maybe call in on Craig's friend John who has a bedsit not far from the hostel, on Stanley Street. Tony might join them, although he is supposed to be on a training

12. This is a miserable arrangement and one that Ann and Kevin are keen to see the back of. With Poppy two months into her job and growing in confidence every day, they have plans to open the hostel on Monday and Wednesday afternoons, although this will spread the staff cover rather thinly.

placement today. Roy has an appointment to keep at the DSS. Paula is going to walk over to her parents' house to fetch some of her clothes while her mum and dad are out. Half an hour later, Kevin closes the hostel, locks up and walks Roy over to the DSS.

At 5 o' clock, when Poppy arrives to work the evening shift, Chris, Paula, Richie, Craig and Tony are all waiting outside the hostel. It has been raining steadily all afternoon and they are soaked through. Everyone heads directly for the front room and the television; Tony makes coffee. Graham and Terry arrive 40 minutes later, by which time Poppy and Chris are nearly done cooking the evening meal.

After dinner, Paula and Siobhan go out together to visit Siobhan's sister. The others pack into the front room to watch the football, all apart from Terry who prefers to sit in the staff office with Poppy, listening to music on his portable stereo. The evening passes quietly with little fuss. An ex-resident calls round to show off her new-born baby, and then, much more exciting, a friend of Tony's visits with a computer game, which everyone fights over. Poppy spends half an hour sitting at the kitchen table with Graham, helping him to draft replies to two letters he has had demanding money, and then spends 20 minutes filling in a housing benefit form with Tony.

By 9 o'clock there is still no sign of Roy. Half an hour later he rings the doorbell, stoned and incoherent; Poppy lets him in on condition that he goes up to bed immediately, which he does. There is a phone call from a London hostel – a referral, a young man called Jonathan, looking to move away from the capital.

The main event of the evening is announced by sirens. An ambulance and then a police car pull up outside one of the bedsit properties across the road from the hostel. The residents press against the front window to watch events unfold. Richie and Craig slip out and bring back a muddled report of a fracas between tenants.

With the fuss over, the evening starts to wind down. Richie plays a few games of draughts with Craig and Tony; Graham and Chris cook up a snack in the kitchen. Paula and Siobhan arrive back in the nick of time, breathless and laughing, just as Poppy is locking up.

*   *   *

Day after day on Lime Street passes much like this. The pace varies, some days are more fraught and frantic, others more subdued, but the baseline tempo is rarely lost. The television is always on and there is always coffee to be made. Weekends mean two whole days indoors, a break from long afternoons spent

hanging around the shopping centre. And then there is the fortnightly cycle of benefit payments: two weeks managing on
dwindling funds and then, on giro day, the chance to splash out
and live a little, to take a trip to the shops or the amusement
arcade as a paying customer and smoke cigarettes from a pack
of 20.

Most days most residents are hard up, and life at the hostel is
correspondingly frugal. This is taken for granted, but it does not
go without saying. Conversation around the table at dinner and
in front of the television turns again and again to money: how
little of it anyone has, how many more days to go until giro day,
and how best to get by until then. However, life on a low budget
at the hostel is not as tough as it gets, as those who have come
to Lime Street from rented bedsit properties already know. At the
hostel there is, at least, no gas meter to keep topped up or fuel
bills to pay, and there is usually enough food in the cupboard to
go round. No one goes without, even those who have fallen
behind on their kitchen money.

No one on Lime Street is ever short of company either. Like all
hostels and shelters for the homeless, the Lime Street hostel is
an active social setting; a composite community of friendship
groups, factions and alliances – twos and threes who have hit it
off with one another, 19-year-olds disdaining to mix with 16-
year-olds, tacitly acknowledged leaders and hangers-on, couples
'going out' together (see Liebow, 1995: 189). The pattern of these
relations gives life at the hostel its tone and temper, shifting and
reshaping with the turnover of residents. Occasionally, for two to
three weeks at a time, the resident group comes together as a
whole, hanging out *en masse* in the town centre during the
afternoons and sitting up late at night packed into one of the
bedrooms, talking.

If the hostel is lively and sociable at its best then it is not
always so, and for some residents it is no fun at all. James is one
of a few who conspicuously fail to fit in and make friends on
Lime Street; an awkward young man, given to talking to himself
under his breath when anxious, he is judged 'weird' on arrival
and is victimised by the resident group throughout his stay. And
it is not just a vulnerable few, like James, who are sometimes left
out or persecuted. Anyone can fall from favour. The social
dynamics at the hostel are fickle, and those who were very much

'in' last week can find themselves 'out' this week, having quarrelled with roommates. Petty disputes between residents are commonplace, starting up, simmering on and fizzling out with every day that passes, and occasionally flaring into confrontations that set the whole resident group on edge. And there are, of course, days when social life at the hostel simply falls flat, days when nothing happens and no one has much to say: residents sit listlessly watching television soap after television soap or fall asleep on the sofa for hours; no one has any cigarettes and the butts in the ashtrays have already been picked apart and rolled up in papers to be smoked again; everyone is broke and there seems nothing to look forward to.

The staff are a part of the social mix at the hostel, for all that they are in a position of authority over the young people coming to stay. Relations between the staff team and residents are generally informal and amicable enough. Staff members share meals, chores and cigarettes with residents and watch television along with everyone else, when they get the chance. The staff office is usually open to residents, and sometimes fills up with an overflow of young people from the front room on busy evenings. When the office gets busy like this and the younger members of the staff team are on duty it can be hard to tell staff and residents apart at a glance.[13]

But the staff are not residents; the hostel is their place of work and their job can be a busy one. The staff member on duty is always the last to bed at night, and must be downstairs before anyone else in the morning to turn off the alarms, unlock the doors and deal with the post. With breakfast out of the way, residents need chasing around the house until the chores are done. Then there are phone calls to make – to arrange for the washing machine to be repaired, to take issue with the social services over an inappropriate referral; appointments to keep – a meeting at the ABC project and then a trip to the magistrates court to speak on behalf of a resident; errands to run – to the supermarket for the weekly shopping. When the hostel opens again at 5 o' clock there may be new arrivals waiting to be shown around and signed in. Once dinner is cleared away, time must

13. Unless they have a meeting to go to away from the hostel, the staff dress casually for work in jeans and trainers.

be found to sit down with residents who have news that they want to share, problems that they want to unload and plans they want to discuss. And all the while the rest of the house has to be monitored, an eye kept on the front door and a stream of petty requests fielded. Can Paula use the office phone to call her boyfriend; can Craig have £1 from the kitchen money tin to buy some more milk and a packet of biscuits; can everyone stay up an extra half an hour to watch the end of the film?

Ann, Kevin, Poppy and Philip work overlapping shifts, and the only time that all four of them are together and away from the residents is at the weekly staff meeting, which is held upstairs in the staff bedroom-cum-storeroom. These meetings run for the best part of two hours. Routine household and practical matters are dealt with first, and then, after a break for coffee, the staff turn to the real business at hand: how best to get the young people presently milling around downstairs settled and sorted out. Each resident is discussed in turn. The common denominator is housing – it is only a matter of weeks until these young people will be leaving Lime Street, and arrangements have to be made to find them somewhere of their own to move on to. But there is much more besides to consider and confer over. Chris' court appearance is only days away; Roy's drug use and Graham's debts need to be worked at; Paula needs to make her mind up about whether or not to go back to college; and as for Tony, Ann's main worry is that, as she discovers over breakfast one morning, 'he doesn't even know how to boil an egg'.

The principal means for addressing any and all of these issues is *key-working*. Residents who stay at the hostel any longer than two weeks are assigned a key-worker: a member of the staff team who will work with them during the remainder of their stay at the hostel, providing practical assistance and support in working towards agreed goals. All residents are required to meet with their key-worker once a week, if only to discuss their immediate housing needs. Graham's key-worker is Poppy, so it is she who accompanies him to court to renegotiate payment of his fines, helps sort out his myriad other debts, and phones up the ABC project to check that he has registered with them and is looking for accommodation. In the weekly staff meetings when Ann asks 'Where are we up to with Graham?', everyone turns to Poppy for an answer.

Key-working is a hit-and-miss affair, however. Plans made in the course of key-work sessions – to start saving for a deposit on a bedsit room or to apply for the job advertised at the supermarket – are not always followed up on, and are all too often overtaken by events: a giro fails to arrive when it was supposed to, or a pregnancy test turns out positive, and everything is thrown into a new confusion. And many residents are no sooner settled in at Lime Street, it seems, than they are off on their way again.

*   *   *

In the space of only a few days, half the resident group has left Lime Street. Richie, Terry, Tony and Siobhan have all moved on to rented bedsit rooms of their own, and Chris has moved back to stay with his mother. These five are quickly replaced by new arrivals.

The first of these is Danny. He is dropped off outside the hostel by his father, who drives off as soon as Danny has lugged his bag from the back seat of the car. Danny has left home under a cloud after one too many calls to his parents from the local police station; he is 16 years old. His family know about the hostel because Danny's sister Clare stayed there a year ago.

The next day three boys call at the front door together, sent over from the ABC project. These three – Ralph, Jason and Nick – have 'done a bunk' from the rented room they were sharing, leaving unpaid bills and some damaged property behind them. They are in high spirits and confident of finding another, larger room to share before long.

As Ralph, Jason and Nick are unpacking their things, a girl called Georgia phones up to ask if there is a vacancy. She has just turned 17 years old and has been staying with a friend since walking out on her parents during a row, over a month ago. She is beginning to feel a bit of a burden, and having rung the social services for advice she has been given the hostel's number. Later that evening she comes over to look around the hostel and talk to the staff. She tells Kevin she will move in at the weekend, but the following afternoon she phones again and says that she has found a place of her own, a bedsit room on Marlborough Hill.

'I was surprised how easy it was to get it sorted out', she says. 'I thought it would be really difficult.'

Danny finds himself sharing a room with Roy. Over the next couple of weeks these two, both 16 years old, become inseparable and a source of continual mischief and disruption around the hostel. The staff team, Ann especially, invest a lot of time and energy into trying to organise suitable accommodation and support for the two of them; a process that entails convoluted liaison with the ABC project, social services and the local youth justice team.[14] Filling in forms with Danny, Ann discovers that he can barely read; keen that he should do something about this, she sets about persuading him to join a local literacy class. Danny is non-committal.

Ralph, Jason and Nick are all 19 years old, and the general feeling among the staff is that these three should bear more responsibility than Roy and Danny for sorting out their own housing. However, a fortnight on from their arrival, they show little sign of doing so. The three of them spend most afternoons driving around in Nick's brother's car, and most evenings partying with friends. On more than one occasion they stay away from the hostel overnight.

When Nick and Jason announce that they are leaving – Nick to return home to his parents and Jason to stay with friends in London – Kevin takes Ralph aside and tells him that he is welcome to stay at the hostel but that there are to be no more nights out and he must start making an effort to find himself some accommodation.

'Don't play at being homeless, Ralph', he says, as the two of them set about tidying the kitchen.

A phone call from the Careers Service reveals that Danny has not been attending the training placement arranged for him, and that, as a result, his benefits have been stopped. Ann calls him into the staff office to discuss this new development. Danny looks sullen; he knows that he is about to be told off but does not quite have the nerve to get up and leave. Instead, affecting insouciance, he drags on his cigarette and flicks the ash on the carpet. Ann takes a deep breath.

'Danny, you've got to understand, you're being catapulted into adulthood. You're going to have to behave like 20 when you're only 16. That starts with not flicking your cigs on the floor.'

Danny goes out later that evening and does not return to the hostel. Two days later he calls in to pick up his bag, telling Kevin that he has found somewhere else to stay.

Three weeks on from Nick and Jason's departure, Ralph finds a bedsit on Victoria Road. He is excited at the prospect of having a place of his own, but has become quite attached to life on Lime Street and is sorry to be leaving. He has been something of a model resident since

14. In the mid-1990s these teams comprised youth justice social workers, employed by social services departments, responsible for a range of shorter-term (sometimes supervisory) tasks with young people who might have offended.

his dressing down from Kevin and wants to know if he can come back to the hostel to help out as a volunteer. Kevin says wait and see.

The day after Ralph leaves, Georgia phones. She has been evicted from her bedsit, and is homeless again.

Against the Grain

The Lime Street hostel deals with its share of difficult young people, at a difficult time in their lives. The staff expect no less, and although residents who are hostile or unruly present a problem and take up a lot of time and worry, they are also often the ones that the staff are most anxious to 'get through to', as Poppy puts it. Giving young people a chance, even and especially those who are hard to help, is very much a part of the hostel ethos: the staff work with difficult young people, that is what they do. It would, in a way, be too easy if the residents were no trouble at all – as Kevin puts it, 'there'd be no challenge'. Instead, it is one of the pleasures of working at the hostel to see young people who were truculent and suspicious on arrival open up over the course of their residency. This is the way things have gone with Richie, by his own account.

> *Richie*: I'm not so angry and I've really calmed down [since first arriving at the hostel]. I suppose a bit of encouragement ... Philip done a lot for me, and, like, I thought, you know what I mean, I don't want to let nobody down and on top of that I want to help myself out. If people are helping me out then I might as well help myself out – kind of buckle down. So I did.

Although the staff prefer to manage the hostel with a light touch, there are times when this is just not possible; those residents they cannot win over must be told. The staff team's authority at the hostel is absolute inasmuch as they can withdraw the offer of accommodation from any resident, without appeal. Staff members moot and threaten this course of action much more often than they actually resort to it; but residents who have been warned repeatedly and who consistently disregard the house rules and disrupt life at the hostel for others living there are sometimes given short notice to quit the premises – a week at most or a couple of days in which to make whatever arrangements they can. Some residents are asked to leave the hostel at even shorter notice. As soon as he has finished fixing up Leon's bloody nose, Kevin tells Shane to pack his bag – violence at the hostel is not tolerated, and Shane must head off to the social services to see what, if anything, his social worker can do for him.

Of course, no one abides by *all* the house rules, at least not all of the time, and minor run-ins between staff and residents are an almost everyday occurrence. Trying to keep ten young people to the lesser domestic arrangements at the hostel is a job that never ends. As soon as Ann has got Cherie vacuuming the front room, the back door will slam as Marky slips out without clearing up the breakfast dishes; Craig goes out to cash his giro and returns to the hostel in the late afternoon with only half of the kitchen money he owes; no matter how many times Poppy reminds residents about the fire regulations, someone is always smoking in the bedrooms at night. The staff take their part in this running battle with a resigned good humour much of the time, but there are days when they find themselves fed up with chasing after the residents.

> *Poppy*: We just hate having to go on and on at somebody. Really it gets to the point where ... [throws up her hands]. They don't realise how we hate having to nag. I mean, they hate us nagging, but we hate doing it.

And the residents do bridle at the nagging and reminders.

> *Shelley*: They treat you like children here ... they're like parents, they just tell you what to do all the time.

But still, Poppy perseveres. There are jobs that need doing around the place after all, and the rules set standards for behaviour, standards that Poppy hopes Shelley will come to make her own. As the staff see it, a sense of discipline and responsibility, fostered on Lime Street, will stand residents in good stead as and when they move on to accommodation of their own. It is because the rules carry this normative freight that staff are prepared to stick to their guns.

> *Ann*: I mean, the aim isn't for us to make life as difficult for them as possible, it's to keep the hostel clean and to make them responsible for cleaning. When we're at home we have to do something every

day ... so I don't think this is being unreasonable or anything, is it? It's just [about] getting responsibility.

Every day offers myriad opportunities for the staff to repeat this message. If residents barge into the office when Kevin is on the phone he sends them out and tells them to knock, 'just like for a job interview'. And if Tara plays her music too loud when others are trying to watch television, then this gives Ann the opportunity to talk

> *Ann*: ... about their boundaries, about respect, about responsibility. All behaviour is useful. You can always reflect it back on them and use it.

But it is this same layering of import that makes breaches of the house rules so exhausting. If all behaviour is useful and significant, as Ann suggests, then the consequences of Marky's refusal to help out in the kitchen always go beyond that of whether or not the washing up gets done. It is the staff team's whole agenda that is being contested in these instances, and this challenge is repeated daily.

Residents who confine themselves to minor-league infractions of the house rules (at least when the staff are watching) can stay at the hostel for the full eight weeks, but they are expected to use this time constructively – exploring their housing options, taking stock of their general situation and considering 'where they want to go in their life' (see page 24). Only not every resident jumps at the chance, and the key-working system, intended to assist and encourage residents in getting to grips with their situation, is not always the co-operative undertaking that the staff would like it to be.

*   *   *

Ann and Marky are in the staff office; this is a key-work meeting. Ann's questions about plans for leaving the hostel are met with shrugs, so she changes tack, trying to persuade Marky to at least think about regulating his drinking and drug use. He says he will try – wants to try – but is non-committal when Ann suggests she make an appointment for him at the local drugs counselling service. Ann reminds him that he has fallen behind on the payment of his court fines.

'What should I do to help you? What would help?' she asks.

'You could lend me a fiver so I can go out and get pissed, then I wouldn't be round the hostel bothering you. No, I'm only joking Ann.'

Ann is exasperated. 'None of this is going in, is it? I want you to show some responsibility, and a willingness to work with us.'

*   *   *

Marky has his reasons for being flippant with Ann, and in context they are good enough reasons. Homelessness is a bruising experience and many residents come to the hostel stubbornly pessimistic about their situation. Fed up and frustrated, they do not always want to hear about how they should be settling down, looking for work and keeping out of trouble. They know this already, and it is all very well for others to tell them what they need to do. If Marky is not inclined to think too long or hard about where he will go when he leaves Lime Street, then this is because he already knows, or suspects, the answer: he will more than likely go back to another run-down bedsit like the one he was evicted from only a few weeks ago. He knows his drug use is getting to be a problem, but it is his problem, to be dealt with when he feels ready (and having just sorted his benefits out for the first time in months, he is looking forward to giro day more than anything else right now).

Marky is 19 years old and has been living away from home for four years, in and out of rented rooms and stop-gap living arrangements; he is a tough nut to crack as the staff see it, fond of him as they are. Those who come to the hostel after only a few days or weeks on their own are not always any easier to help. Jack, 16 years old and still at school, is distracted and restless in his key-work meetings with Poppy. Glad to be gone from home, and even a little thrilled at the precariousness of his situation, he is confident he will land on his feet as and when he decides to 'get things sorted', and is not to be persuaded to start setting money aside for a deposit on a rented room just now.

Ann and Poppy have worked with dozens of young people like Marky and Jack and they expect to have to chip away at them. All the same, it is something of a puzzle and frustration that some residents don't seem to want to help themselves. Occasionally the staff team worries that life on Lime Street is a little too comfortable. The hostel offers two months' accommodation, rather than two weeks or only a couple of days, so as to give residents time and 'breathing space' (see page 23), but this is intended as more than an extended respite from homelessness. If Marky is not too bothered about looking for accommodation or sorting out his court fines, then the staff can't but wonder if the hostel is somehow letting him off the hook. Sometimes these anxieties are acute.

*   *   *

Staff members have been finding things difficult at work of late. The feeling is that too many young people are 'using' the hostel without really taking advantage of the help that is on offer there. Kevin, for one, feels that the staff have been a little too easy on the residents, especially the younger ones, some of whom need to be taken in hand a little more, made to see the seriousness of their situation and appreciate what it is that the staff are trying to do for them. Yesterday was a tough day for Kevin. His attempt to get residents involved in a local five-a-side football league ended badly when the hostel team turned up for their first match drunk. The game was a farce, deteriorating quickly into a series of scuffles. The residents' participation in the league is now over.

This morning the staff team are discussing their concerns with Brian, a member of Southerton Housing's management committee. Kevin launches into an account of the football match, but Brian is keen to get to what he feels to be the heart of the matter.

'I think football on a Thursday afternoon is OK, but if I'm homeless and unemployed I want to get my life together, don't I?'

'They don't though', insists Philip. 'They rebel against anything you try.'

Philip has been having a tough time of it at work too and, like Kevin, he is starting to feel that things need to change. He would like to see residency at the hostel conditional upon participation in a programme of constructive activities. 'Something like that, anyway. Right now too many of them are just using the place – like Scott, like Jenny. If they're not playing the game then we shouldn't hang on to them.'

'I think that we do need more structure, finally', says Ann. 'I do feel that, and I think it's going to take a while for us to sort out what it is we want to do. I think we seriously need to sort out our priorities. Two months is not enough time to do all the things that we want to do with people but it is enough time to home in on what their priority is, which is accommodation. I think it's indicative of the problem that

Matt has been here seven weeks and only last week did he go and look at some accommodation.'

'Well it shouldn't be like that', says Kevin. 'If it's like that, then there's something that we're neglecting in the area of structure and discipline.'

Ann reminds the meeting that, as of next week, the hostel will be open to residents on Monday and Wednesday afternoons (something she and Kevin could never stretch to when there was just the two of them on the team). She suggests that once this happens there will be more time to work with the young people like Matt.

'Right now I only see him for a few hours each week, and then everything's manic and people want their tea and what have you. In the afternoons we'll have more time.'

Poppy is anxious though. She wonders if this is the right thing to do, with the residents as they are just now.

'That attitude, the attitude I've sensed is that they almost feel that they're doing us a favour. You know, they've got it easy here; they don't realise how easy.'

Brian has reservations too. He wants to know what the staff plan to do with the residents all day.

'If they're sat in the lounge doing nothing, watching TV, then that's not enough', he tells Poppy.

'But Brian,' says Ann, 'that's what they'd be doing if they were in a bedsit. What can they do? There is no daytime provision in Southerton at the moment; there's no work for them at the moment. Would I rather have them sitting in the lounge doing nothing or out jimmying Astra locks? That's the choice.'

'Well that's their choice, not your choice', says Brian.

*   *   *

Every few months the staff find themselves having a conversation like this, agreeing that the time has come to get tough with the residents and make some changes around the place. And sure enough, for a week or so 'structure and discipline' will be the new watchwords on Lime Street – the house rules inflexibly policed, key-working sessions brisk and businesslike. But this new regime never really feels right and always unravels. Running a tight ship is one thing, but the staff are not at the hostel just to order the residents around. They are there to help. And helping is an open-ended, collaborative exercise; it takes trust, time, humour and reciprocal understanding as much as anything else. It is a muddy exercise too, inscrutable sometimes. An hour spent patiently reasoning with Marky might seem like water off a duck's back at the time only to pay dividends, unexpectedly, somewhere a few days, or months, down the line; Shelley's six weeks' 'dossing' at the hostel might, deep down, be just what she needs right now.

And then again it might not. These are the imponderabilia of helping, and they come with the territory. However much of a relief it is, at the end of a long shift, to sound off about residents who are not playing the game and to draw the line between

Philip: ... people who want to be helped and people who can't really be bothered, people who are going to be pissing us around ...

no one really wants to pick and choose. And Philip knows as well as anyone that the residents slide in and out of these categories from one day to the next. Those who were disruptive at football yesterday are apologetic and co-operative this morning; those whose attitude is all wrong today might yet wake up to themselves before they leave.

Leaving

Residents leave the hostel whenever they are ready to do so, and by the end of eight weeks at the latest. Most of them move into rented bedsit accommodation in and around Southerton's town centre, of which there is no chronic shortage (although see pages 48–55). A few move elsewhere: James to tied accommodation along with a job in the kitchens at an out-of-town hotel; Keith to a bail hostel in the next town; Bagsy to a YMCA (Young Men's Christian Association) hostel, two stops away on the London train; Georgia to a council-run mother-and-baby unit; Jonathan to a drug-rehabiliation unit on the south coast. Every so often residents leave the hostel to move back in with their parents, even those who arrived on Lime Street insisting that they would never even speak to their parents again. Craig is one such, enjoying home comforts again after seven weeks at the hostel and a month in a cramped bedsit on Victoria Road.

Craig: I would have gone home before if I'd had the chance, but I'd said some really nasty things to my stepmum ... but my mum [remarried and living locally, but with no room for Craig] came to see the house I was in and she told my dad what a dive I was living in, and it got me home [i.e. back with his dad and stepmum]. And life's so easy really, innit, living at home. My stepmum didn't really want me back cos she didn't really believe I'd changed, but me and her get on really well now. But I'm moving out again, if I can.

Others would go back if they could – Marky would go 'like a shot' if his mum would have him home again. Aimee says she won't go back, even though her mum has asked her – 'too stubborn', she explains; Andy has not seen or spoken to his mum and dad since the day he walked out on them, six months ago; Rhys has no close family – 'none that I know of, anyway'. Cherie's relations with her parents have thawed a little in recent months to the point that she phones to chat and tell them how she's getting on every now and then and has visited once, for an afternoon; but this renewed entente is too fragile (and precious) to be put to the test. As she sees it, staying apart is the only thing that will keep her and her parents together, and so she plans to find a place of her own somewhere.

> *Cherie*: I've been away from home nearly a year now and it would be hard, like, going back … I know I'd probably end up leaving again and that would be, like, that would be it between us, and there'd be nothing between us again. It isn't worth taking that chance.

Wherever it is that young people go when they leave Lime Street, it can be a bit of a wrench to have to say goodbye to friends and familiar routines. Most leave with mixed feelings. When Matt packs his bags after seven and a half weeks on Lime Street, he is sorry to be leaving but glad to be gone all the same. The hostel was a godsend at first and he has enjoyed living there much more than he ever thought he would. He will miss the buzz of the place, 'the company and that', but he has had his fill of weekday afternoons spent hanging around outside waiting for 5 o'clock to come around; the house rules have started to chafe too, and the lack of privacy and personal space has been getting on his nerves. Having found a small bedsit room on Catherine Street, five minutes' walk away, he is looking forward to having somewhere of his own – with his own key; somewhere he can get up when he wants and do as he pleases.

The staff, for their part, are generally pleased to see any young person leave the hostel, provided that they 'leave properly, and move on to having a more stable lifestyle' (see page 23). Leaving properly means leaving preparedly, with one's priorities straight and one's life in some sort of order. Richie's departure is a case in point. Headed for a good-sized room in a housing association property and carrying a box of pots and pans that the staff have got together for him he is as ready as he'll ever be. His benefits are in order (for the first time in several months) and he has worked out a weekly budget with Ann; the DSS and his probation officer and solicitor have been notified of his change of address. His court appearance, only a few weeks away now, is the next big hurdle. Ann and Philip will be there to speak for him, and he is determined, whatever happens, that it will be his last time in front of the magistrates.

Some residents exit the hostel sooner than the staff would like. When Ryan announces his departure only a week on from his arrival on Lime Street Ann and Kevin have their reservations. Pleased with the initiative he has shown in finding himself a room, they can't help feeling that he is rushing things a little. Ryan has only £9 to his name and another whole week to wait until his next giro. He is only 16 and has never lived on his own before, and Ann's attempts to talk to him about the new responsibilities he will face – cooking, cleaning, budgeting, bills – do not have the sobering effect she was hoping for: Ryan insists he will be OK. His flippant suggestion that he will shoplift food in order to save money for drugs does nothing to allay her anxieties.

Ann and Kevin suspect that this will not be the last they see of Ryan. And there would be nothing new in that. Not all those who leave the hostel are gone for good or, for that matter, for long. When Kevin gives his usual pep talk to departing residents, helping them load their bags into the boot of his car, he tells them the hostel has done its part and that now it's up to them:

> Kevin: Let's see how you do out there. We'll see how you do on your own ... we're going to challenge you and see what happens.

If he never hears from them again then that's fine, he says, and if they want to call by one day next week and let him know how they're getting on then that's fine too. But he knows very well that some of those he drives across town to their new accommodation will be homeless again and back on Lime Street soon enough. Ryan very probably, quite possibly Cherie, and perhaps even Richie.

3
In the Bedsits

The only local accommodation available to young, single people on a low income in Southerton is in private rented rooms at the bottom end of the housing market. Even here rooms can be hard to come by. Most local landlords prefer 'reliable' tenants who have regular jobs that will take them out of the house during the day, and are similarly wary of letting to young people, particularly 16- and 17-year-olds, who are felt to be 'trouble'. All the same, there are some advantages in letting to unemployed teenagers, so long as the demand for accommodation is there. The council's money – housing benefit, paid directly to the landlord – is as good as anyone else's and young tenants effectively excluded from the rest of the housing market are easily fobbed off when it comes to complaints about damp rooms, peeling wallpaper and dodgy electrics. A modest property with a mattress on the floor of each of three rooms upstairs and two more rooms downstairs, a lock on each door and a shared bathroom and kitchen can be quite a lucrative venture. A handful of landlords in Southerton have made this particular market niche their own, letting almost exclusively to young people on benefits.[1] This is where about eight out of every ten of the hostel residents end up.

The rooms on offer are generally cramped and shabby, and sometimes much worse. At the slum end of the market they can be dirty, damp and even infested. Richie has stayed in several such properties, all owned by one, notorious, local landlord.

> *Richie*: Mate, you don't want to know what his places are like. They're disgusting. When I was living where Andy is staying now there was cockroaches running up the walls, and mice. Honestly, it was disgusting. The kitchen was disgusting and the bathroom was foul.

Accommodation in rooms like these is a precarious business, rarely subject to any legal agreement. Tenants may be evicted

1. Not all young people are welcome however: 'No jungle-bunnies or kids with rings through their nose', as one landlord put it to me, bluntly.

with little or no advance notice given; threats and harassment from landlords are not uncommon. Bagsy is another who knows this end of the housing market only too well.

> *Bagsy:* Southerton is full of arsehole landlords; they screw the youngsters for everything they've got round here. Especially ——; if you piss him off then he gets his fucking mob to do you over. He thinks he's the king on top of the castle around here.

But not all Southerton's landlords are crooks and bullies. Nor are all cheap bedsits as bad as those that Richie talks about; a few are quite decent. In any case, after a couple of months spent sharing rooms at the hostel a bedsit of almost any description can be welcome enough.

As elsewhere throughout Britain, flats and bedsits to let in Southerton are advertised on cards in shop windows and, every week, in the local newspaper. Many of these advertisements are marked 'Sorry no DSS', but there is usually one, maybe two, worth following up on. The ABC project is a consistently useful point of contact – it acts as a clearing house for information about local accommodation and holds a register of landlords willing to take tenants on housing benefit; callers can usually be found accommodation within a couple of weeks.[2] In fact, the principal obstacle to securing a rented bedsit room in Southerton is not availability, although this is certainly limited. The big problem is money. Almost all landlords ask for either a cash deposit or a few weeks' rent paid in advance before they will allow a new tenant to move in to a property. The amount requested varies, but is rarely less than £100. Needless to say, this sort of sum is well beyond the immediate means of almost all the young people who come to stay on Lime Street.

Although staff members at the hostel regularly encourage young people to use their stay on Lime Street as time in which to save for a deposit on a room, residents are rarely able, and not always inclined, to set aside enough money from their benefit payments. And so, when a young person is reaching the end of

---

2. The ABC project is also a regular source of referral to the hostel. The two organisations work closely together, the hostel acting as a holding operation of sorts, providing temporary housing to young people in emergency need of accommodation while the staff at the ABC project try to find them somewhere more permanent to stay.

his or her stay at the hostel and has found a room to move on to there usually follows a scramble to find enough money with which to secure the accommodation. A small number of residents feel able to turn to their parents for help at this point and others have probation officers or social workers who can sometimes be persuaded to provide financial assistance. The majority, however, must go into debt; the most common way of doing so is to apply for a crisis loan from the DSS.

*   *   *

After a month at the hostel Terry moves to a rented room close to the fast-food restaurant where he works part time. Six weeks later his landlord phones the hostel to say that Terry has disappeared owing £150 in rent and can consider himself evicted. The staff can offer little explanation as they have not seen or heard from Terry for some time. However, sure enough, Terry turns up the very next day. He is a likeable, shy young man with mild learning difficulties.

Terry tells Ann that he has been sacked from his job because he could not keep up with the pace of work in the kitchen. Unable to pay his rent, he has been staying with a friend for the past week, trying to decide what to do. Ann phones Terry's landlord, who relents and says that he will take Terry back, on housing benefit this time, but only if he first hands over the £150 he owes. Terry, however, is broke – he has already been to the DSS to start his claim for benefit, but he will not be getting a giro for another week. He spends another night at his friend's house.

The following day, after further negotiations between Ann and Terry's landlord, it is agreed that if Terry can get a crisis loan from the DSS to cover at least £100 rent in advance he can move back in immediately and make good his debts at a later date. Terry is actually not all that keen to go back – he says that the room he was in was tiny and the house was a mess; but he cannot stay with his friend indefinitely and so he heads off to the DSS. He returns 15 minutes later having been put off by a receptionist who has told him that he will not be eligible for a crisis loan as he is not actually homeless. Ann takes Terry back to the DSS to speak to the social fund officer, who eventually agrees that Terry is probably eligible, but points out that, as he spent last night at his friend's place some distance out of town, his case is the responsibility of a different office.

The next morning Kevin, Ann's deputy, drives Terry to the other DSS office only to be told, once the forms have been filled in, that

Terry cannot have a crisis loan as there is not enough money left in the local budget. That afternoon, back at the hostel, Kevin rings Terry's probation officer to see if she can help, but she also says that her budget is exhausted. Terry says that he used to have a social worker and that maybe she could help, but he cannot remember her name and it proves difficult to find anyone at the social services department who will acknowledge him as their responsibility, despite a series of increasingly irate calls by Kevin. Terry will not contact his family to ask for help – he has not seen or spoken to them for several months.

After another night at his friend's house, Terry goes back to the Southerton DSS office and, on Kevin's advice, tells them that he has spent the night sleeping rough in the town centre, making his application for a crisis loan their responsibility. The social fund officer has no means of checking this story, and so, as there is enough money in the budget in Southerton, Terry gets the loan. He moves back to his old room the following afternoon.

*   *   *

Desperate though they may be, Terry's experiences here are no more convoluted than those of many other of the young people passing through the Lime Street hostel. The search for money with which to secure rented accommodation is almost always difficult and stressful, and not always successful. However much of a last resort, the DSS is no certain source of funding: many of the hostel's residents have their crisis loan applications for rent in advance turned down.

Although the workers at the ABC project prefer not to deal with Southerton's less reputable landlords, their clients can't always afford to be so choosy. If a young person needs accommodation in a hurry, for whatever reason, and there are no immediate vacancies on the ABC project's list, then the best bet is usually to turn to the landlords that Richie and Bagsy complain about. These landlords need no persuading to consider housing benefit – they expect nothing else – and will sometimes be flexible about asking for money in advance, settling for £30 up front, for example, and then half of next week's giro as a 'deposit' which is unlikely ever to be returned. The movement of tenants in and out of the rooms at the very bottom end of the rented sector also means that vacancies come up here more frequently than elsewhere.

Moving into a new room is the work of an hour or less for most of the hostel residents as Southerton is not a large town and most of the cheap rented accommodation is clustered together in a network of streets, all within walking distance of Lime Street. Few of the young people leaving the hostel have more than a couple of boxes of belongings; a single trip is usually enough to transport a resident's entire possessions to his or her new home. This may make unpacking a quick and easy task, but it invariably leaves the rooms still looking rather bare; most are only sparsely furnished to begin with, with a bed or mattress and one or two mismatched pieces of second-hand furniture. The hostel is sometimes in a position to help out here, distributing donated furniture to ex-residents living nearby; and the young people themselves, those who settle in a new room for any length of time, usually make small additions and alterations to the general decor week by week. The most prized and, in its way, essential accessory for any bedsit room is a television.

There is, however, a limit to what can be achieved on a social security income, and rooms that have been occupied for some months can continue to look rather spartan and dingy despite the best efforts of those living there.

*   *   *

Vicky lives on Stanley Street, a busy road close to the town centre. She rents a single room in a house of multiple occupancy, sharing the kitchen and bathroom with four other tenants. Her room is furnished with a bed, a small sofa and a chest of drawers. A second-hand stereo system is stacked against the wall in a corner of the room and on top of this is a black and white portable television. In the absence of any posters, scribbled graffiti – 'FUCK THE SYSTEM', 'VICKY LOVES JONES', 'SPLIFF UP' – covers the walls. The room is lit by a bare light-bulb hanging from the ceiling.

Vicky has lived in this room ever since she moved from the hostel a year ago. In all this time she has never signed a tenancy agreement and has never seen any of her rent, which is paid directly to her landlord by the local council. She gets on tolerably well with her landlord; he lends her small sums of money whenever she is short and has overlooked the fact that, for two months now, she has been sharing the room with her boyfriend, Jones. All this is set to change however. Vicky has complained to the council about a leak in the roof and today there has been an inspection. Her landlord is extremely displeased; he has been told that he must make substantial alterations and improvements to the property if he is to continue to rent to multiple occupants. Whether or not he acts on the council's recommendations, he has made it clear to Vicky that she must find somewhere else to stay by the end of the month.

Tracy also lives on Stanley Street, opposite Vicky. She has a bedsit room in a small terraced house. Although she has only lived there for a couple of months, having moved from Marlborough Hill and before that from Lime Street, Tracy is leaving today. She has never liked the room, which is very small and smells damp, and has recently fallen out with one of the other tenants in the house. I am helping her with the move. We pack all her things into nine plastic carrier bags and walk across town with them, Tracy glancing over her shoulder every hundred yards or so, worried that we will run into her (ex) landlord – she has not told him that she is leaving, and owes him money. Her new room on Victoria Road turns out to be larger and altogether more pleasant. It has been recently redecorated, albeit hastily, masking the worst of the wear and tear of a succession of previous occupants. She sets to unpacking her things – clothes and shoes mostly, a mug and kettle and a few pots and pans, two posters for the wall and a stuffed toy. She has no bedding other than a sheet and a sleeping bag, which she unzips to make into a blanket of sorts.

Tracy tells me that Roy has recently moved into a room upstairs. We go up to see him but he is not home. A pair of jeans on the radiator and a dirty ashtray on the floor by the mattress are the only evidence that his room is occupied.

*   *   *

Moving from emergency hostel accommodation to a privately rented room of one's own, however modest, might seem like a significant step out of homelessness and housing worries. It is certainly a move that many of the hostel residents make with some sense of excitement and optimism, especially those who are moving to a place of their own for the first time. However, this enthusiasm seldom lasts more than a few days. Many of the hostel residents struggle, almost from the outset, to manage on their own in bedsit accommodation. Some are wholly unprepared and unequipped for independent living. Roy, for example, moves from Lime Street to Victoria Road with no more than a single change of clothes stuffed into a black bin-liner. He has no kitchen utensils or bedding of his own and little idea about how to cook, shop and clean for himself. Quickly disillusioned, he spends no more than a week in his new bedsit, eating take-away meals, before quitting the room altogether and returning to the serial, stop-gap living arrangements with which he had been making do before he first came to stay at the hostel.

Despite the best efforts of the staff team, many residents leave Lime Street little better equipped and able than Roy. But, important as they are, skills for independent living are not the real difficulty. The root problem facing almost all those leaving the hostel is the boredom and confinement of life in bedsit accommodation on a low budget. Days when nothing much happens are slow enough at the hostel, but alone in a single bedsit they can drag on for what seems like forever. With nothing to do all day and very little money, even those who are much better prepared than Roy and who have been lucky enough to secure decent rooms find living in the bedsits tedious at best, and utterly miserable at times.

> *Samantha*: I've got to get some music or a TV, that room's driving me mad. I'm just sitting there staring at the walls. I've got to be really careful who I have round cos the police have told me if I get in trouble again I'm going to get it in the neck. So I'm staying out of trouble but it's driving me mad. I can't tidy the room cos I've done that already. I'll just have to go back and have another bath. I'm seriously thinking about asking my Dad if he'll have me back, cos I'm just going nowhere.

This is Samantha, who was, at first, 'made-up, really made-up' to have found a place of her own, a good-sized room in a shared house, but who now wishes she were anywhere else. Young people as bored and miserable in bedsit accommodation as Samantha is rarely stay for long. Some pack up and leave without any definite idea about where to go next other than to take up a half-promise of a few nights on a friend's floor. Some, like Tracy, swap rooms, flitting across town to a different house in the slender hope that things will be better, or different at least, in a new room. A few are evicted from their accommodation following some or other dispute with its roots in the same dissatisfactions that make them want to leave anyway, and have no option but to move on. In serial combination these alternatives make for a pattern of unsettled residency in a succession of bedsit rooms, interspersed with temporary, stop-gap living arrangements. Roy and Vicky are at different ends of this spectrum, Roy lasting only a week before vacating his room, Vicky facing eviction after twelve months at the same address. In between these two, most of the young people moving on from the Lime Street hostel do well to hold on to a fixed address for more than three months.

Money Matters

Hard up as residents at the hostel undoubtedly are, when they move on from Lime Street their financial difficulties are usually only just beginning. Cash may be needed for a deposit, more than can easily be set aside from a fortnightly social security income, and various essentials for setting up home must be bought if they cannot be borrowed (although, often enough, they are done without). Living away from the hostel, money is tighter – cooking for one is more expensive, and there are usually bills to pay over and above what housing benefit covers.

Getting by on the dole requires the careful management of a limited income. Once the bare necessities of life have been budgeted for there is precious little left to spend. And, as many of those moving into bedsit accommodation are already in debt, not least for the money they have had to hand over to secure their accommodation in the first place, they have even less room to manoeuvre than most. Even those who somehow manage to start out with a clean slate find it all too easy to slip up and fall short, running out of money two or three days before their next giro is due. When this happens, as it often does, money must be borrowed – perhaps £5 from a friend, for tea and milk and cigarettes – against the promise of repayment on giro day. Inevitably, this means that the following two weeks' money is even less likely to go the distance. In this way, in a matter of months, some find themselves operating almost entirely in arrears. Jones routinely spends his giro day handing over money to various creditors – friends at the hostel, a local drug dealer, his auntie and myself – leaving himself, at the end of the afternoon, with almost nothing. The next day he is borrowing again, promising repayment in two weeks' time.

This is an extremely precarious and unenviable position to be in, and accepting the logic that those barely keeping their heads above water ought not to make waves one might expect Jones, and others like him, to practise a careful, anxious economy. But in fact, although Jones spends many hours fretting over how best to make do on the limited income available to him, he is also, often, a spendthrift. The same is true of many others. For any young person stuck in the same dowdy bedsit for days and weeks on end the temptation to get out of the house and spend £10 in the games arcade, or twice that amount on a night out, can be hard to resist. Occasionally the lure of a few hours' real indulgence proves altogether too much and two weeks' money is squandered in a single afternoon, spent on designer sportswear, or drugs, or fruit machines, or CDs, or any other combination of consumer pleasures, leaving bills unpaid and debts still owing. Those who are least settled in their accommodation, and especially those who find themselves between rooms (i.e. homeless again) on giro day, take even less persuading to spend what they have there and then.

Whether squandered today or set aside for tomorrow, social security ought at least to be a predictable income, the next instalment never more than two weeks away. But repeated moves between different rented rooms, and other changes in circumstance, mean that many of the young people's claims do not run at all smoothly. The arrival of an official manila envelope with the morning post invariably brings on an intense anxiety that something has gone wrong somewhere along the line, and as often as not this turns out to be the case.

*   *   *

I have borrowed a car for the day and Shane, Robby and Gary all want lifts. Shane and Robby both need to go to the DSS as their social security claims are messed up. Shane started his claim when he was still (supposed to be) at school, and although he has not attended regularly for the best part of a year he has only recently passed school-leaving age, as a result of which his conditions of entitlement have altered and he must reapply. He should have done this last week. Robby is also in difficulties: he has had a letter telling him that his benefits have been stopped altogether as he has missed an interview for a training placement; he claims that the letter notifying him of the interview never reached him. We drive to the DSS, where Shane collects new forms to fill in. Next we drop Robby off outside the Careers Service, leaving him to argue his case with them.

Gary's situation is somewhat different. His giro did not arrive at his bedsit yesterday, and after a morning spent at the DSS he has now been issued with a replacement. He has not told the DSS, but he thinks it likely that the original giro was in fact delivered to a previous address and so we drive over there to see. Twenty minutes' drive brings us to the house. We pull up outside and Gary gets out and rings the bell. After an argument with the live-in landlord, he comes back to the car triumphant: he now has two giros. Driving back, Gary and Shane weigh up the risks and rewards of cashing both; Gary decides to give it a go.

*   *   *

Many of the hostel residents get into difficulties with their benefits almost as soon as they move away from Lime Street, particularly the 16- and 17-year-olds, whose social security income is dependent on their being registered with the Careers Service as available for training. Some – Robby is one such – seem to lurch from one crisis to the next, their claims in continuing disarray, unsure when their next payment is due and whether it will arrive at all. Those who slip back into stop-gap living arrangements and episodic homelessness sometimes lose track of their claims altogether and go without any income at all for several weeks at a stretch.

The most common cause of disruption to social security payments is a failure to inform the DSS about a change in circumstances. Needless to say, it is not in the young people's interests to jeopardise their own income, and their apparent negligence here owes more to a lack of understanding about the claiming process than it does to laziness or indifference. Despite the fact that social security provides a financial lifeline for almost all of those moving on from Lime Street, hardly any of them have anything approaching a clear and thorough understanding of how the system works. Instead they are intimidated by, and unpractised at, dealing with the bureaucracy; they find the application process tedious and confusing and the rounds of the various offices onerous and time-consuming, and they have only a slim appreciation of the consequences of failing to meet their obligations as claimants. Shane, Robby and Gary, and others like them, are very much focussed on the here and now. Once in receipt of social security, they prefer to give as little further information to the DSS as possible for fear they may somehow lose out financially as a result or prompt some bureaucratic adjournment. Most of the time, and especially for those whose accommodation is in flux, all that really matters is getting hold of this week's money. Once this has been achieved tomorrow's obligations – an appointment at the Careers Service, say – may be postponed or forgotten; the next giro is now two weeks away and a lot may happen between now and then. Needless to say, short-cuts and petty deceits such as Gary is considering lead, in time, and inevitably, to long delays.

When the system catches up with them there is little to do but to traipse round to the DSS and face the music. As often as not they come away none the wiser as to why they must start their claim all over again. 'I'm off the guarantee list, whatever that is', says Debbie when her benefit is stopped because she has not attended the training placement arranged for her. 'I ask them what these things mean but they never tell me.'

Unsurprisingly, attitudes towards the DSS and, by extension, the Careers Service and JobCentre are overwhelmingly negative. At worst these offices are seen as representative of an impenetrable bureaucratic process with the seemingly capricious power to either grant money or withhold it without explanation.[3] Most of those in the bedsits adopt an accordingly cynical – instrumental – attitude towards social security. Few of them claim to feel any strong moral obligation to play fair by the system; almost all are willing to 'blag' some money if they can get away with it.

*　*　*

Billy is broke and desperately wants some cash. His benefit income has been erratic of late and his next giro is not due for several days. He goes to try and wheedle some money from the DSS, telling them that

3. Pat Carlen finds the same 'weary cynicism about both those who make the rules and those who enforce them' (1996: 115) among young homeless people interviewed in Manchester, Birmingham, Stoke-on-Trent and Shropshire.

he has been evicted from his bedsit and has nowhere else to go as the hostel is presently full. His story is a fiction, but he is nonetheless indignant when his request for an emergency payment is turned down.

'I don't care what the book says', he shouts. 'Look at me! I haven't had any money for two weeks.'

Outside the DSS Billy continues complaining. Cherie suggests that he goes back in and applies for a crisis loan for toiletries and underwear; she says that this worked for her when she was staying at the hostel. Billy gives it a go, and it works: he gets £20, which he then spends on some cannabis and a music cassette.

*   *   *

Benefits are a constant preoccupation. Everyone has stories to tell about current difficulties and past injustices, and sometimes the occasional triumph; but few make any attempt in all this to present themselves to one another as good claimants – honest and actively seeking work, in contrast to more mercenary, undeserving others. On the whole, and amongst themselves, the feeling is that if someone can get something out of the DSS then they have earned it. It is suggestive that the receipt of a giro is usually referred to, without much more than a touch of irony, as 'getting paid'.

As far as the world of work is concerned, the young people leaving Lime Street are novices. Lacking in confidence, qualifications, experience and resources – a home telephone, a set of smart clothes – they have little idea where or how to begin looking for a job. Most are busy enough dealing with the vagaries of the benefit system and have no immediate plans to complicate things further by looking for work. It does not help that the limited opportunities available to the young unemployed in Southerton are, for the most part, in part-time or temporary jobs that scarcely offer to replace money already received in benefits.

*   *   *

Andy, an ex-resident, calls in at the hostel to share his good news: he has been offered a part-time job as an office cleaner. He will be working two and a half hours a day and earning £45 a week; best of all, he will have to wear an official-looking security tag to work, and is busy filling this in at the kitchen table. He is aware that his new income will mean a drop in the level of his benefit payments, but even so he expects to be about £30 a week better off. For the past two months he has been paying £20 out of every giro to an ex-landlord to pay for damages to a property he once stayed in, and this has left him hard up and in debt to various friends: £30 a week would make a big difference.

Later that day, at the DSS, Andy finds out that if he takes the job he will lose almost all his social security benefits. He will be only £15 a week better off, and his housing benefit payments will be affected too. He is too despondent to look into how much housing benefit he might lose. For a couple of hours he considers not declaring his new income at all, but he eventually decides this would be too risky.

'If I get caught I'll only have to pay it off, and I've got enough debts as it is.'

The next morning he phones his new employer to say that he will not be taking the job. He asks if there is any full-time work going, but is told no.

*   *   *

The net result of these occasional, miscarried forays into work is that few of those in the bedsits spend much time looking for work at all. Some are brazenly pessimistic about their chances, like Barry, who cheerfully insists that he and Gary are 'just dossers ... we're unemployable'. Others keep their expectations on a tight leash, insisting that jobs will come, but later, 'when I've got myself sorted out'. Either way, those who find themselves called to interview at the JobCentre to discuss their search for employment are often forced to concoct a list of spurious applications made, in order to satisfy the interviewing officer.

Those who do look for work, and who manage to find a job that they feel they can afford to take on, do not always last long in employment.

*   *   *

Graham and Yvonne meet at the hostel and fall in love; together they make plans to move out into a place of their own. On a Tuesday evening they go to see a bedsit room for rent in a house just round the corner. They like the room, but the landlord tells them he wants a cash deposit and will not take housing benefit. Neither Graham nor Yvonne is working. Graham has been claiming benefit since he left home, owing money to his parents, four months ago. In that time he has accumulated over £300 in debts 'on the catalogues'; he also pays £15 a fortnight in court fines. Yvonne is only just out of school and has not claimed benefit before. She is awaiting a decision on an application for Income Support on grounds of 'severe hardship'.[4] They tell the landlord they will think about it.

Encouraging one another, Graham and Yvonne start looking for work. On Thursday, Yvonne is offered a temporary job in telesales that pays £4 an hour. Returning to the hostel to tell Graham, she finds he has been out all afternoon drinking with Jones, who received an unexpectedly large, backdated giro that morning. Graham and Yvonne have their first row. The next day the argument is forgotten and they are chasing up an offer of a double room in a house near to where Barry and Patrick are living. The landlord also wants money up front, but he will take housing benefit. Graham and Yvonne are very enthusiastic, although they have not actually seen the room. They spend much of the afternoon back and forth between the hostel and the DSS arranging a £110 crisis loan for rent in advance (repayments to be docked at source from Graham's benefits). On Monday they go to meet the landlord at the property to see the room and to hand over the giro cheque. The room is so mouldy and damp that they reluctantly turn it down and return the giro to the DSS the next day.

On Wednesday, Yvonne starts her job. Graham has an offer of work too, as a porter in a warehouse. The job is for four weeks only, the hours are 1.00 p.m. to 11.00 p.m. weekdays, 7.00 a.m. to 3.00 p.m. weekends, and the warehouse is some distance away. That evening they phone to ask if the bedsit in the house round the corner is still available. It is, but the landlord wants a £100 deposit, not rent in advance, before he will let them move in. Crisis loans are not issued for deposits on rented property, and so Graham resolves to phone his mum and dad.

'They'll help me now that they know I'm working', he insists, hopefully.

His parents agree to lend him the money on the condition that he promises to repay the £200 he already owes them. Graham and Yvonne are thrilled. On Friday Graham goes to see his parents for the first time since he left home. He returns to the hostel wearing a new

4. A discretionary provision applying to certain young people aged 16–17; today, Yvonne's application would be for Jobseeker's Allowance, again on grounds of severe hardship (see Child Poverty Action Group, 2002).

pair of trainers and with only £50, not the £100 he was supposed to have. He borrows £40 from another resident, Michael, who has just cashed his giro, and the landlord settles for £90. Graham and Yvonne move into their new place: a smallish, ground-floor room, mostly taken up by a double mattress.

Yvonne goes to work on Monday to find that her job has gone – she is not clear why exactly. She gets £98 pay and buys a pair of trainers like Graham's. On Thursday, Graham quits his job because the hours and the travel are keeping him and Yvonne from seeing one another – he is jealous of the time she spends in the evenings at the hostel, visiting. He has been offered some work locally, cash in hand, with a friend who fits carpets; but when he goes to see about this it turns out that there is nothing for him and so he is unemployed again. The DSS do not know about the warehouse job, so Graham hopes that his fortnightly giro will arrive as usual next week. Even so, this will hardly be enough money.

'Rent is £50, and I've got to give my mum £20 a fortnight – that's for the loan for the deposit on this place. Then I've got court fines to pay and money on the catalogues, £71 on one and £269 on the other. I need to speak to the landlord. He still thinks I'm working; I don't know if he'll take housing benefit.'

Graham and Yvonne let things slide a little over the weekend, spending the last of Yvonne's money. By Monday they are broke. Graham goes to collect his wages for the hours he worked at the warehouse and is given a cheque, which he cannot cash as he has no bank account to pay it into. He calls at the hostel to see if Michael will wait for his money, and after some discussion he gives Michael a jacket, which they agree will cover £15 of the debt.

Yvonne applies for benefit again (wishing she had never told the DSS about her telesales job). Graham and Yvonne call in to see me, Yvonne has forms to fill in.

'I need to sign this before I go up to the office again, I've got to see them for an interview. Am I down as "Yourself" or "Partner"?'

'Partner', says Graham.

'You see, he won't let me claim for him. I don't want to be "Partner", I think the giro should be in my name. I don't think it's fair. I think we should pick it out of a hat.'

'You do it then', Graham snaps, explaining to me, 'She doesn't trust me with money.'

'I'm not saying that', Yvonne insists. 'I'm not saying anything.'

Two weeks later, Yvonne calls at the hostel asking if she can stay the night. She is thinking of leaving Graham. The two of them have been getting on each other's nerves; they have no money, they are stuck indoors all day, and Graham does not help out with the tidying up. The following morning she goes back to the bedsit and tells him she is moving out.

Graham stays on at the bedsit – his landlord agrees to take housing benefit – but he is not happy living on his own. Depressed about his debts, he spends most of any money he can get getting drunk. Yvonne finds a place of her own on Stanley Street: another bedsit, one that Marky was recently evicted from. She has new forms to fill in to notify the DSS of her change of circumstances and has no plans to look for work again anytime soon.

*   *   *

Graham and Yvonne's story is about more than work; it is about a complex of financial and other difficulties, alongside which work takes its place as just one more (short-lived) source of worry and frustration.

Hours and Days

If time were money, unemployed teenagers living alone in rented bedsit accommodation would be as rich as Croesus. As it is, the daily, hourly, challenge they face is to find some way of making the time pass. Household chores can fill up only so many hours each day, in addition to which there may be appointments to keep at the DSS, the magistrates court or the social services department; but this still leaves the greater part of every week blank. Few are prepared to sit out this remainder on their own, waiting for something to happen.

The hostel provides some respite here. Almost all of those leaving Lime Street call back at the hostel from time to time. Some are back within a matter of hours, declaring themselves to be at a loose end and wanting to know if they can watch television with the other residents in the front room for a few hours. Visits to Lime Street are also reciprocated. Residents step out in the evenings to call on friends who have moved on to nearby rented rooms, slipping back in later, woozy with drink or dope. On midweek afternoons when the weather is wet the bedsits provide a ready shelter from the rain, somewhere to hang out until the hostel opens up for the evening.

Those in the bedsits also keep each other company, calling in to catch up on the news and pass the time of day. Most of the cheap rented accommodation in Southerton is clustered together in a small grid of streets, and so ex-residents often find themselves living only a few minutes away from one another. Occasionally, a row of houses or a single property comes to have the feel of a Lime Street satellite – filled with tenants who know one another from previous stays at the hostel.

* * *

Three weeks after Tracy moves to Number 10 Victoria Road Tony follows suit – he has been staying in a house full of older tenants, several of them alcoholics he says, and is glad to get out; he takes the room recently vacated by Roy. Tracy has started a romance with Ed, who has the room next door to hers and has lived on Victoria Road for six months now; Tony and Ed already know each other slightly, and in the space of a week these three become inseparable. Number 10 is now the place to be. In the evenings, residents from the hostel and other of Tracy and Tony's friends living nearby get together in Ed's room to play video games, of which Ed has a large, much-envied selection, and smoke dope.

Melanie is a regular visitor – she knows Tracy and Tony from when they were all residents together at the hostel a year ago. She has lived on Victoria Road too, at Number 74, but was evicted after a row with another tenant and has been living with her boyfriend and his parents for some time now. One day she calls at Number 10 in tears; her boyfriend has been arrested for breaking into a local shop, and his parents have kicked the two of them out. As a favour, Ed moves in with Tracy, letting Melanie and her boyfriend have his room until they can get something sorted out. This is a somewhat risky arrangement as Number 74 and Number 10 belong to the same landlord and he will not be pleased if he discovers that Melanie is staying at one of his properties again. Melanie keeps a low profile and after a few days she and her boyfriend move back in with his parents.

A week later Tracy calls in at the hostel looking to borrow a pint of milk and meets Owen, who has come to Lime Street from a hostel on the outskirts of London. She invites him over to Victoria Road and, as he is voluble and generous with his cigarettes, he soon makes himself popular with Tony and Ed. There are seven rented rooms in Number 10, and when one of these is vacated three weeks later Tracy lets Owen know. He gets a crisis loan for rent in advance from the DSS and moves in.

Owen has been at the house for less than a week when Tracy and Tony call in at the hostel to speak to Ann. They say that Owen has broken into the gas meter and Tracy is worried that if and when this is found out they will all be in trouble. Ann persuades them to go and see their landlord to let him know what has happened. Owen is duly evicted and disappears back to London.

Ann arranges for Al to move from the hostel into Owen's old room. Al is only just 16 and, like Roy, whose old room (now occupied by Tony) is across the hall, he finds it hard living on his own; he misses life at the hostel. After only a few days on Victoria Road, he asks to move back to Lime Street but Ann persuades him that he is better off trying to make a success of living independently. Things brighten up for Al when Shane is evicted from the hostel following a fight with another resident. Shane and Al used to share a bedroom on Lime Street and now that Shane has nowhere to go Al puts him up on his floor. With Al and Shane both at Number 10, the house becomes even more of a hot spot. In the evenings Al's room is full of stoned 16-year-olds watching television with the sound turned down and listening to music on a stereo borrowed from Tony.

Al and Shane get into the habit of spending the afternoons shoplifting in the town centre; the police call at the house several times looking for the two of them. This does not go down well with Ed, who deals drugs on a small scale and is understandably nervous about police visits. Tony, Tracy and Ed are quietly relieved when, after a month spent at Number 10, Al is evicted for having failed to pay a single one of his weekly bills. With Al and Shane gone the house is much quieter. Tracy finds a part-time job, cash in hand, working in a café for a few hours most evenings. She does not encourage people to come round as much as she used to. Things have also soured between her and Ed somehow and the atmosphere in the house is not the same.

One afternoon, a fortnight after Al's departure, I meet Tracy on the street and she tells me that Tony has moved out unexpectedly.

'He don't want anyone to know where he's moved to. He's got a lot of stuff going on in his life – he needs to get himself sorted out', she explains, enigmatically.

As it happens I know more about Tony's whereabouts than Tracy does. Tony is sleeping on the floor of my bedsit, at Number 74 Victoria Road (Melanie's old room); he has been staying with me for a couple of days. He claims that Ed has turned against him for no obvious reason and that he does not feel comfortable staying at Number 10 any more. He plans to lie low for a couple of days and then move back to the hostel, if there is a vacancy there and they will take him back.

*   *   *

There are advantages and disadvantages to finding a room in a house like Number 10. It beats being stuck on your own in a house full of strangers, but it can also be tiresome and claustrophobic in much the same way as life at the hostel gets tiresome and claustrophobic after a while. And however animated life may appear to be in properties like this, most days, as is the case for almost all those in the bedsits, there is little or nothing doing.

Hearsay and drugs are the staples of bedsit sociality. Sitting around the television watching children's programmes in the late afternoon, or getting together to pass the time in the evenings, there is a continual round of small talk and speculation about recent events. For those who have been stuck indoors all day the smallest item of news from the outside world is eagerly seized on; those who are new on the scene and have a story to tell can always be sure of an audience.

The ebb and flow of tenants through properties like Number 10 Victoria Road, and the shifting relationships that accompany this movement, offer plenty to chew over. Small talk in the bedsits often takes the form of a running commentary on the personal fortunes of others: who's in, who's out, who's 'lost it', is 'going downhill' or has 'landed on her feet'. Burgeoning romances are always gossiped over; break-ups and recrimination are more interesting still.

Friendships among those leaving Lime Street tend to burn brightly but quickly: feuds between one-time associates are common. Thrown together at the hostel and then at Al's bedsit, Al and Shane are as thick as thieves, but a month after they have moved on from Victoria Road they are no longer hanging out together and are trading insults and threats through intermediaries instead. There is rarely all that much behind these sudden animosities: money borrowed and not returned; a favour withheld; a minor betrayal of some sort; a forgotten grudge, stirred back into life by those with no business meddling. Long days stuck indoors provide fertile ground for the spread of spurious allegations. Tracy is forever making mischief in this way, and is probably behind Ed's sudden turn against Tony. For those on the sidelines, these public fallings-out make for entertainment of a sort, a topic for discussion and speculation; but for those directly involved and on the receiving end they can be a tense and miserable business.

When there is little to tell that is all that new, favourite events and incidents from months past are revisited: Suzanne's weekend away with the Prince's Trust, where she turned a profit selling, as amphetamine, medication she had been given for a urinary infection;[5] Scott's run-in with the police in the town centre; Tara's overdose. If the principal proponents are not on hand or cannot be encouraged to give the story again, others willingly step in. Marky is a consummate bedsit performer, able to reel off elaborate re-enactments of past incidents and encounters – his own and other people's – in a sort of one-man pantomime of impersonation and improvisation. It does not matter much that his stories are unreliable, the details reworked and elaborated in the retelling; as long as the performance is convincing, listeners are ready to suspend disbelief. Inept or improbable boasts may be met with derision, but more often than not, and especially on those days when the hours are dragging by, the ability to make something from nothing is a welcome one (see Corrigan, 1993). Some accounts are fabrication from the outset, notably Tracy's far-fetched and tragic autobiography, which she regularly reinvents. Yet every now and then what seems an unlikely story turns out to be closer to fact than fiction. Mandy's claim to be on the run from a London drugs gang sounds overblown, until the door to her friend's room is kicked in by four strangers who then set on the young man when he refuses to say where she can be found. Derek's insistence that he is in line for an inheritance seems equally dubious; but who knows for sure?

Drugs are much more a feature of life in the bedsits than they are at the hostel where staff members are on hand to police the premises. Cannabis – dope – is an almost everyday accompaniment both to the solitude and the sociality of days spent with nothing much to do. Hour upon hour, alone and in company, are whiled away sitting on the edge of a mattress with reggae, rap or hip-hop on the stereo, rolling and smoking skinny joints. Either this or, when someone has money, an all-night session spent getting high with friends, eventually 'crashing out' surrounded by a litter of apparatus ingeniously constructed out of drinks containers, tape and tubing. As well as being something (fun) to do, drugs constitute a shared consumption niche with

5. The punchline: ' ... and some of them came back for more!'

its own vernacular and paraphernalia, within which one can be knowledgeable, expert and experienced. Drugs are not cheap, but a good time can be had at home smoking dope, or talking away nineteen to the dozen on amphetamines, for less money than would be spent on a night out drinking in a pub or club. Some even manage to make a little money out of drugs, although far fewer turn a consistent profit than claim to be able to do so.

> *Tara*: I'm making some money soon. I'm going to be dealing, just to friends – buy an ounce with my giro and then sell it off by the eighth at fifteen quid a time.

Drugs bring problems too – trouble with landlords, hassle from the police, disputes and debts and ill-health. This is especially the case with hard drugs such as crack cocaine and heroin, which are used by only a small minority of those passing through the hostel. The regular use of hard drugs with the possibility of addiction and dependency is generally looked down on. Those using drugs other than cannabis or amphetamines with any frequency are usually cautious about letting this be known.

> *Shane*: I'm no druggie. I don't let any one know I'm doing it [crack cocaine], I always buy off different people. I don't have a habit or anything, I can go without it, but if I've got the money then I'll buy some and get wrecked.

Shane is playing a more dangerous game than most of his peers, for whom drugs are a pretty ordinary kind of fun, just something to do and a reason to get together.

*   *   *

Craig and Luke crashed out at Vicky's bedsit on Stanley Street late last night, having spent the evening getting high and watching television with Vicky and her boyfriend, Jones. Craig knows Jones from when the two of them were residents at the hostel, several months ago. No one really knows who Luke is – he only arrived on Lime Street a week ago and more or less invited himself along to Vicky's, but was welcome enough as he had money to spend. This morning, when I call by, Jones is still asleep on the sofa. Luke is sleeping too, wedged between the bed and the wall, with his coat draped over him. Craig is making tea for Vicky, who has been up for several hours waiting for her giro to arrive. As soon as I walk in the door she asks me if I have seen the postman.

After a further, anxious wait of half an hour, Vicky's giro drops through the letterbox. Jones wakes up, puts on his shoes and a jacket, and he and Vicky head into town to cash the giro and treat themselves to breakfast together at a café. Craig and I walk down to Lime Street together to have a coffee and watch television, leaving Luke still sleeping. A couple of hours later, Jones and Vicky come and find us at the hostel. They are both in high spirits having eaten well, settled debts with Vicky's dealer and got some amphetamine 'on tick'. We walk over to the police station together where Craig has an appointment to receive a caution for an incident in the town centre a few weeks ago. Next, we call in at the games arcade. Vicky gives Jones and me some money to play a few games of pool, Craig wanders into the back room where he meets Jack, Shane and Jono who are watching someone play the latest Formula One video game. After an hour or so all seven of us head back to Vicky's bedsit (there is no sign of Luke, who has, presumably, gone back to the hostel). The next few hours are spent, as so often at Vicky's, smoking joints, drinking tea and coffee, listening to tapes and playing cards. It is sunny outside, but we keep the curtains closed.

Talking about anything and nothing, at one point the conversation shifts to mention of Al (whom Shane is bad-mouthing) and this jogs Jono's memory. A while back, midway through an evening at Al's old bedsit on Victoria Road, Jono gave Shane £15 to go and buy some dope. Shane took the money, but never returned, later claiming to have been stopped by the police on his way back and had the cannabis confiscated.

'Oh yeah, hold on', says Jono. 'You owe me fifteen quid.'

'No I don't. What for?'

'You stitched me up a treat. The other night, at Al's.'

'I told you: I was arrested, wasn't I. So I lost it', says Shane, sticking to his original story.

'I know you didn't. You went round to Marky's and smoked it – he told me. So you owe me fifteen quid, thank you very much.'

Shane is flustered for a moment. He starts to shift the blame to Marky, and then promises to settle up with Jono once he has managed to collect the money that Graham owes him. Jono quickly loses interest; it seems unlikely that he will see the £15 again and he does not want to make a scene.

With the afternoon coming to an end, Vicky starts to get anxious about how little money she has left. Breakfast at the café, drug debts, the trip to the arcade and a couple of packets of cigarettes have cost her over £40. She owes her landlord £10, and unless she can somehow avoid paying this she will have only £20 to last her for the next two weeks. Her shoes are coming apart at the heels and she is trying to persuade Jones to buy her a new pair when he gets his giro next week.[6] Jack and Jono decide to head back to the hostel for dinner, promising to come by again later in the week when Jack 'gets paid'. Jones, Shane, Craig and I wander down to the shopping centre looking for something to do, leaving Vicky watching television on her own. Shane is still banned from the centre following a fight with the security guards earlier in the year, but the guards do not recognise him on this occasion and we are let in. Inside we meet Billy, who was recently evicted from the hostel but has now found himself a bedsit in a property belonging to one of the less reputable local landlords. He plans to have people round this evening for a housewarming 'session', and we agree to meet up there later on.

*   *   *

For every memorable afternoon or evening spent passing the time with Jones and Vicky on Stanley Street, or partying at Number 10 Victoria Road, there are many, many more days spent alone and in the doldrums: sitting in silence through a morning's television, getting up and down every five minutes to adjust the aerial; drinking another cup of tea and wondering whether to go window shopping in town; drifting back to bed in the afternoon to kill a few hours, hoping that someone will call round with cigarettes. These days are deadly. Yet time spent in company can grow tiresome too. Marky, outwardly one of the more upbeat and irrepressible of those passing through Lime Street, is not the only one to feel, sometimes, that the best of times in the bedsits still fall a long way short of what he wants and feels he is missing out on.

> *Marky*: I need to get out of bedsit land. I need to be somewhere else, not in the bedsits. You just get lonely and bored all the time ... friends come round and you just want to get caned [high] to make the time pass more quickly.

For Marky, afternoons spent getting high and careless with friends, once a welcome diversion, are starting to feel like a part

6. Vicky and Jones receive their benefit income independently of one another; they have not told the DSS that they are living together.

of the problem. He is caught between a rock and a hard place, unhappy on his own and in a crowd, and wants out of 'bedsit land' altogether. In Marky's case these reflections are the likely prelude to another of the spectacular solo drug binges that have disrupted his accommodation several times in the past year. Others feeling the same way find their own settlement or catharsis. Some drop out of sight and circulation for a while and turn in on themselves, staying indoors and not answering the door; some turn on one other.

*   *   *

This evening Jones and Vicky call round to my place on Victoria Road. We sit and drink cans of cheap lager for a while and then go out to get cigarettes. On the way to the shops we meet Craig. He walks with us to the off-licence and buys some more cans, which we then decide to take back to Vicky's. When we get there Jones and Craig, slightly drunk, start a mock fight, rolling around on the bed together. Vicky is annoyed and insists that Jones tidies the bed now that he and Craig have messed it up. Jones refuses, and suddenly an argument flares up. Vicky raises her voice; Jones tells her to fuck off; she loses her temper and throws an ashtray at him; and then they are at each other, pushing and shoving. Jones says that he is leaving and walks to the door, but Vicky grabs at him, scratching his face badly. He hits her, very hard across the face, and she falls backwards onto the bed, stunned. Craig and I get in between them and I walk Jones out of the house, leaving Craig to look after Vicky.

Jones and I walk down Stanley Street. He is angry and upset and insists that he is leaving Vicky for good.

'You see what she's like Tom? I can't live with that, it's doing my fucking head in. She's just lost it. I'm not going back there. Fuck that.'

He asks if he can stay with me for a night or two, and we start to walk over to Victoria Road.

'She's mad. Like the other day I went out to get a loaf of bread and I ended up staying out for most of the day like, and when I got back she was cutting up her arm. She needs help man. She's fucking crazy. What was all that about? Just over who was going to make the fucking bed. It makes you laugh. I don't want to go back there. All her friends are criminals and I'm trying to get out of all that. They're all criminals, man. And her dealer's always round – any time we have a row she's always straight down to her dealer's. When I first moved in I thought I could help her, but fuck that. She's out of control, man. She's always going on about how she's had a hard life, but she's not had it hard, no way man. My dad used to beat the shit out of me every night almost. She hasn't had it hard. It might be all right if I could get her away from here, but as long as she's living in Southerton there's no fucking chance she'll change. I don't like to hit her, but she fucking asked for it.'

By the time we reach my house Jones has calmed down and thinks that he should perhaps go and see if Vicky is all right. We turn around and start to walk back together.

*   *   *

Vicky and Jones are not the only ones who struggle to stay happy sharing a single bedsit room. When they first got together they were crazy about one another, and deciding to live together felt like one of the most exciting decisions either of them had ever made. A few months on they are still in love, Vicky insists, but they fight a lot and the room on Stanley Street is not the cosy, intimate refuge it was when Jones first came to live there. The reasons for this are manifold, but the room itself is at, or close to, the root of the problem: it is the room they would change if they could change anything.

Out of House and Home

The absentee landlords who rent out so many of the bedsit rooms in Southerton are not picky about who lives in their properties or what they get up to as long as the rent is paid and there is no trouble. When there are problems at a property, however, they brook no nonsense and are happy to clear a room out at short notice to make way for new tenants. Evictions are commonplace and are rarely, if ever, contested. Only very few of those in the bedsits have ever signed an occupancy agreement in the first place, and fewer still are aware of their rights as tenants. Most who are told to leave simply set about clearing out their rooms.

Notice to quit is often issued with more or less immediate effect – a week's grace is generous; and this means that those 'kicked out' of their bedsits are placed in real and immediate difficulties. Finding a new room is usually the work of a few days at least, and with perhaps only 24 hours' notice in which to vacate a room there is little that can be done. Many of the young people who come to stay at the Lime Street hostel, new arrivals and familiar faces alike, are homeless because they have been abruptly ordered out of a rented room with little or no time in which to make alternative arrangements.[7]

But for all that they may be sudden, evictions do not always come out of the blue. Some young tenants have only a precarious hold on their accommodation from the outset. Al, for example, was never going to last all that long at Number 10 Victoria Road; it was really only a matter of time until he left or was asked to leave, and he knew it. There is also sometimes a sense in which, calamitous as it is to be suddenly out on the street, an eviction is not always entirely unwelcome. No one plans to be evicted, but some do force the issue or, by default, allow their tenancy to slip away from them, relinquishing their hold on rooms that they were never very happy in. To allow oneself to be overtaken by events in this way can be strangely liberating: homeless again, one can start over, leaving behind whatever debts, difficulties and anxieties one has been struggling with at an old address. It is almost a relief to have nothing much left to lose.[8]

Those who have had enough are sometimes just waiting for whatever it will take to bring things to a close. The particular and immediate reasons for eviction are variations on only a handful of themes: unpaid bills; one too many complaints from neighbours about noise and anti-social behaviour; damage to property; trouble with the police.

7. Not that there is any more security of tenure on Lime Street, even in the short term. All new arrivals at the hostel sign an occupancy agreement, but this is a circumscribed document, tailored to the provision of shared emergency accommodation, and as such it does not protect residents from summary eviction for breach of the more serious of the hostel rules – as happens to Tara (see page 76).

8. Compare George Orwell, who writes of the 'feeling of relief, almost of pleasure, at knowing yourself at last genuinely down and out. You have talked so often of going to the dogs – and well, here are the dogs, and you have reached them, and you can stand it. It takes off a lot of anxiety' (2001: 79).

*   *   *

Having shared a bedroom at the hostel for over a month, Cherie and Tara agree to get a place together when they leave. Excited at the prospect, they set about looking for a room and quickly find one among the many flats and bedsits on Marlborough Hill. The landlord tells them that they can move in immediately if they each agree to pay £5 a week, for the first two months, towards a deposit.

Cherie and Tara's new room quickly becomes a popular venue, with residents at the hostel and other young people calling in to hang out during the afternoons and evenings. Two of Tara's friends, Dean and Tariq, call at the house almost every day and generally stay late into the night, playing music and smoking cannabis, to the growing annoyance of some of the other tenants in the house.

Having received several complaints, Cherie and Tara's landlord tells them that they are not to have visitors in the evenings and that Tariq and Dean are banned from the property; but his warning has little effect and the two boys continue to visit. Five weeks into Tara and Cherie's tenancy their landlord calls at the house to find Tariq and Dean on the stairs exchanging insults with a tenant who has asked them to keep the noise down. He demands that the two boys leave – which they do, promising to return later that night to break the windows. This proves to be an idle threat. All the same, Tara gets a letter the next day telling her to leave the premises. She returns to Lime Street, complaining that she has been unfairly singled out as the troublemaker in the house.

With Tara back at the hostel, the staff team hope that things will be quieter on Marlborough Hill and that maybe Cherie will settle down. They are encouraged to hear that she has found a job working as a waitress at a pizza restaurant in the town centre; but the job does not last. Cherie is fired when, after two weeks of juggling late nights and morning shifts, she fails to turn up to work one day.

Having signed off benefits during her brief period of employment Cherie now has to reapply for benefits. Waiting for her new claim to be processed, she falls behind on the instalments on her deposit. Her landlord tells her that she is skating on thin ice, but Cherie is not too bothered; she is not all that enthusiastic about staying in the room now that she is on her own. Dean and Tariq continue to call round (late at night, sneaking in through the window rather than risk running into the landlord again) and Cherie is glad of the company, but the pace of life with these two is starting to get on top of her. She has been taking a lot of drugs and looks the worse for it: unwell and overtired.

Keen to start again somewhere, but not sure where to go or how to leave, Cherie's hand is forced when the police call at the house at 6 o'clock one morning looking for Dean and Tariq in connection with a reported burglary. Her landlord calls later that morning and tells her that she must be out of her room by midday.

Cherie calls at the ABC project in tears, and then at the hostel to speak to Poppy. Poppy is keen to contact Cherie's landlord to see if he might be persuaded to let her stay for another week perhaps – time enough in which to find another room; but Cherie insists that she has had enough.

'I don't want to go back into the bedsits. I think that's where I'm going wrong – in the bedsits. Cos whatever bedsit you go to there's always someone doing drugs and trouble and stuff. I don't want to get involved in that sort of thing again. Whenever I go in a bedsit I always go wrong.'

She moves back to the hostel.

*   *   *

There is not always all that much to choose between those who are evicted and those who quit their rooms under their own steam. Those who are told to go are often just about ready to leave anyway, and those who decide to move on are sometimes only a small step ahead of the landlord. An eviction may be more traumatic and pose a greater risk of homelessness, but many of those who are kicked out of their accommodation are back in another rented room after only a couple weeks spent on a friend's sofa. And choosing to switch rooms is not without risks. Rushed decisions to move sometimes backfire badly, leaving a young person with nowhere to go other than to head back to the hostel.

In summary then, for an assortment of ordinary and desperate and obvious reasons, young people leaving Lime Street struggle to find themselves at home and happy as bedsit tenants in houses of multiple occupancy. About half of those who are rehoused in this way are on the move within a matter of months, trading one tenancy for another nearby, or homeless again. This pattern – shifting back and forth between cheap rented rooms and returning to the hostel *in extremis* – is one that some of those who pass through Lime Street cannot seem to shake, and amounts to a continuing, episodic homelessness.

4
On the Streets

Although there is little visible street homelessness in Southerton
– no cardboard cities or rows of sleeping bags in shop doorways,
not everyone who is indoors at night has a place of their own.
Only a few of the young people moving on from Lime Street to
local bedsit rooms stay settled for long. Some move through a
succession of tenancies in different properties, and there is
nothing too wrong with that perhaps. But others are in real
housing difficulties and homeless again soon enough. Of these,
some return to the hostel for a second residency, another month
or more in temporary, emergency accommodation. Others enter
into an interstitial existence, with no fixed address, sleeping on
friends' floors mostly. Young people who are between rooms in
this way are closer to the street than most, living out of a carrier
bag or with nothing more than the clothes they stand up in and
uncertain from one day to the next where they will be sleeping.
Yet even under such difficult circumstances, most manage
somehow without having to spend their nights out in the open.

*   *   *

Leaving the room she shared with Cherie on Marlborough Hill, Tara
returns to Lime Street. Her second stay at the hostel ends abruptly
when, having taken some medication belonging to another resident,
she collapses in the kitchen and is rushed to hospital. The medication,
it emerges, has been swiped from a locked cupboard in the staff office
along with some money and valuables. The two residents responsible
for the theft are evicted, and the staff team decides that Tara, who was
in on the deal if not personally responsible, will not be allowed back
either.

Tara is kept in the hospital overnight for observation and then
discharged, fully recovered. Unable to return to the hostel, she stops
for a couple of days with Melanie, at her boyfriend's parents' house,
and then, when this arrangement falls through, with Tariq at his bedsit
on the outskirts of town. A week later she is back on Lime Street,
staying with her new boyfriend Paul, in a house directly opposite the

hostel. This is a temporary arrangement. Paul's live-in landlady is sympathetic to Tara's predicament but does not want her sharing Paul's room for any more than a week or two. As things turn out it is only a few days later that Tara calls at my bedsit asking if she can store some things with me – a suitcase and three carrier bags full of clothes – as she has split up with Paul and is moving out.

Over the next couple of days Tara hangs out with her friend Emma, who has absconded from the local children's home. No one knows for sure where the two of them are sleeping at night, possibly with Emma's auntie. The workers at the ABC project set about trying to find some permanent accommodation for Tara, but the problems she had at Marlborough Hill make things difficult. Tara is not impressed.

'They're fucking useless over there', she tells me when she calls to pick up a change of clothes. 'They're not helping me at all. They say that no landlords will take me cos that bastard [her ex-landlord] has told the other landlords not to have me.'

I meet Tara in the park one evening. She has been sleeping on sofas and floors for two weeks now and is worn out and at a loss as to what to do; Emma is back at the children's home. She tells me that the ABC project is trying some family reconciliation work, to clear the way for her to go home to her parents. She is not enthusiastic, but does not see that she has all that many options.

'I wouldn't ask my stepmum, but I was thinking if I went to see my dad he might let me back home. Cos I'm his own flesh and blood, like.'

Two days later, Tara finds herself a bedsit in one of the shabbier properties on Catherine Street, just around the corner from Marlborough Hill. She stays there for the next few months, and then leaves to move in with a new boyfriend.

*   *   *

Not everyone who wants, or needs, to come to stay at the hostel is able to. Tara is in the relatively unusual position of being banned from the premises, but there are plenty of other occasions when the hostel is simply full, with no room available. Under these circumstances other temporary arrangements can sometimes be sorted out at short notice. A few phone calls to hostels and night shelters in nearby towns may locate a vacant bed; the social services also operate a local lodgings scheme, providing young people with overnight accommodation in registered family homes. But these options are not all that popular. Many young people would rather not travel out of town to a hostel they have never heard of, or stop overnight with a family they do not know, and instead they opt, like Tara, to stay on home ground and rely on their own resources and networks.[1]

Those who have not stayed at the hostel before (and may not even know of its existence) and who have fewer friends to fall back on than Tara does are at a greater risk of finding themselves literally roofless. A small number of those who arrive at the hostel for the first time do so having already experienced short spells on the streets. Graham is one such (see page 19); Alan is another – referred to the hostel by the social services, but nervous about moving in, he stayed away for a week, stopping over with friends and sleeping rough, until his social worker brought him to the front door in person. Almost all those who have spent nights out in the open have done so on their own and out of sight. Graham slept in a garden shed, others have spent a couple of nights trying to sleep in a quiet corner in the car park or on a bench at the far end of the train station platform. Most common of all is for a young person to have spent a night wandering the streets having walked out during a row with their parents too late in the day to make any other arrangements.

Richie is one of only a few who have ever had to sleep rough for more than two or three nights at a time. Speaking from the relative comfort of the hostel, he tries to make the most of the time he spent on the streets and the know-how he accumulated:

> *Richie*: I've been on the streets at Christmas before ... really cold, just like this. I'd be able to survive in this and some people wouldn't. I know places to go and that. You try and find empty houses and if you can't find an empty house you find a garage. And when you've got a garage you've got to go out nicking food and that ... You see shops, like any shop round here which sells sandwiches, yeah? What

---

1. Under some circumstances the staff would much rather this than that a young person move to hostel or similar accommodation. When Tracy rings the hostel to announce that she has broken up with Ed and is leaving Victoria Road, Ann spends half an hour on the phone trying to talk her out of coming back to Lime Street: 'It's a backward step Tracy ... it's not good for you to stay here.' When Tracy turns up at the front door an hour later Ann tells her that she cannot stay and that if things are impossible with Ed she should stop with friends for a few days until something can be sorted out. This is a difficult decision, made in what Ann intuits to be Tracy's best interests. Tracy is furious: 'Right, I'm homeless then am I? Thanks for that. I suppose you like making people homeless do you?'

you do is, at six or seven in the morning, you walk round and you see a big, black bin-bag full of bread on the street, waiting for the shop to open – you get those. And then you get loads of milk off doorsteps, cos milk's good for you. Then you go down the sports centre for your shower, so you're still looking reasonably clean, in a way. Then you go to the shopping centre to nick clothes. It's best to nick the ones with the tags on cos nobody watches you then cos they think you can't nick them, but you just rip the tag out. It leaves a hole, but, you know what I mean – clean clothes like, innit?

In a similar vein, Bagsy will talk about how he is more streetwise than many of the other residents at the hostel as a result of having been homeless in central London. But in general there is little credit to be had from having slept rough. It is more often a guilty secret, not something to boast about having been reduced to.[2]

Most of the residents on Lime Street equate homelessness more or less with rooflessness and would not describe themselves as 'really homeless' at all other than when arguing their case for a crisis loan at the DSS.[3] The 'winos' – the handful of older down-and-outs and heavy drinkers who sometimes shamble through the town centre, who may or may not be sleeping rough but fit a familiar stereotype – are the real homeless and the hostel residents do not see any similarities between themselves and these characters, other than in jest.

> *Craig*: The first night I got kicked out, I went and got really, really pissed. I thought: 'Right, I'm fucking homeless. I'd better get used to being pissed all the time.' I didn't know what the fuck to do.

2. This is especially so for the young women passing through the hostel. Shane and Al may feel able to brag a little about 'roughing it' in the days immediately after Al loses his bedsit on Victoria Road, but Tracy would be ashamed to let on to any but her closest friends that she has spent time on the streets.
3. Most young people, following popular and media definitions, consider 'real' homelessness to mean sleeping rough – although Hutson and Liddiard note that 'even young people sleeping rough may not necessarily view themselves as being homeless!' (1994: 29). That the young people coming to stay on Lime Street generally reject the term 'homeless' as applied to themselves can doubtless be understood, at some level, as an attempt to distance themselves from a label they find to be disempowering and stig-matising, and perhaps to 'call into question the categorizations imposed upon their accommodation status by contestants who appear to be fighting the homeless battle way above their heads' (Carlen, 1996: 72).

Craig's recollections of the night he left home are tongue in cheek, but the joke is an uneasy one. Life on the streets with the winos is not pleasant to contemplate and there is little empathy with, or sympathy for, these characters among the hostel residents.

Out of Doors

If, at the end of each day, the majority of the young homeless in Southerton have beds or sofas to go to, at the hostel or elsewhere, they do nonetheless spend a good part of every day on the streets. On weekdays when the hostel is closed from morning until evening residents must spend the intervening hours out of doors if they cannot make other arrangements. Similarly, those who are relying on friends to put them up for a night or two are often out of doors during the day, not wanting to crowd their hosts and wear out their welcome too soon. Those who have moved on from the hostel 'successfully' and have a place of their own for the time being are not so hard pressed perhaps, but the bedsits exert their own necessity and there are plenty of times when the urge to get out of the house and do something to escape the boredom becomes overwhelming.

Young tenants are always popping in and out of the rented properties along Marlborough Hill and Victoria Road on their way somewhere – to the newsagents or into town, or down to the DSS or the magistrates court just to see what is going on. Lime Street is often busy too. When the hostel is closing up for the day or about to open for the evening, residents and friends gather outside, making plans, sharing news and cigarettes and passing the time.

*   *   *

Robby is sitting on the wall outside the hostel and looking anxiously up and down the street – it is a sunny, dusty morning, already hot. Robby's younger brother is rumoured to have 'grassed' to the police about a recent assault on a police officer by a young man called Sean who is trying to build a reputation locally, and Robby has been threatened with a beating if he does not persuade his brother to withdraw his statement. The front door to the hostel is ajar and Robby is ready to scoot back inside if need be. Scott, who recently moved out from the hostel to a bedsit of his own, arrives to give Robby some company and protection. The two of them share a cigarette. Gary, who shares a room at the hostel with Robby, is around the corner at the DSS with Jones, trying to get some money.

Al and Shane turn up brandishing court summonses, which they have received following a shoplifting spree of a few weeks ago and a more recent incident in which a police car was vandalised. They are being deliberately blasé about their impending court appearances, tearing the summonses up and throwing them into the road. Al was evicted from his bedsit last week and has been sleeping in a car parked outside his mum's place. Shane, who used to sleep on Al's floor, is now homeless too; he is wondering if the staff at the hostel will let him stay again as he was only recently evicted for fighting on the premises. Both Al and Shane have been wearing the same clothes for several days. Al's face is thick with grime and he still has a bit of a black eye from when he was beaten up over a fortnight ago.

Jones comes back beaming. Yesterday he was not so happy – flat broke and owing money to both his landlord and his dealer, he had called to collect his giro only to be told his benefits had been stopped because he had changed address without notifying the DSS;[4] he kicked up a huge row, but was told that nothing could be done until the morning. Having spent the whole of yesterday afternoon borrowing money here, there and everywhere – eventually scraping enough together to keep his dealer happy – he has now restarted his claim and been issued with an emergency giro for £33. This is enough to pay off the remainder of his debts, but it leaves him with nothing and puts him 'on the scrounge' again. He is planning to sell the TV that the staff at the hostel recently donated to him and Vicky.

'Mad, innit?' he comments, on everything and nothing in particular.

Gary gets lucky too. He is issued with a £14 crisis loan, having invented some story about being threatened with eviction over debts for damaged furniture at the hostel. Frank, another resident at the hostel, has also been to the DSS, but he has nothing to show for his efforts. He comes back very bad tempered, stringing together all sorts of implausible reasons as to why he should have been given

4. The last address at which Jones was registered for benefits was deemed unsafe for postal deliveries; since moving in with Vicky he has continued to claim from this old address (neither he nor Vicky wanted to complicate things by starting a new claim as a couple, which might mean delays and slightly less money); this means that Jones' giro has continued, up until yesterday, as 'personal issue' – to be collected in person.

something, trying to convince himself, if no one else, that he was in the right. Robby starts laughing at him and Frank takes his jacket off, ready to fight, knowing that the others will step in before anything happens, which they do.

Cherie and her friend Samantha come by and stop for a cigarette; they are on their way to the Careers Service. Cherie's benefit has been stopped because she has not taken up the offer of a place on a training scheme. She is confused.

'I don't remember getting the letter', she says. 'If I got the letter I must have thrown it away cos I didn't understand it.'

* * *

On this particular morning Cherie and Samantha are not short of options. The stage is set for a possibly dramatic showdown between Robby and Sean, Gary has £14 to spend and may choose to be generous with it, Al and Shane are at a loose end and can be fun to hang out with; sorting out Cherie's benefits will, in any case, take up a good part of the morning. But the prospect of a day spent out of doors is not always attractive. Mick, Alex, Shelley and Barry, all residents at the hostel, are underwhelmed at the options as they see them on a cold and wet autumn morning.

Mick: Get stoned; doss around town; try and find a job.

Alex: Find a place to live.

Mick: Just bumming around really.

Shelley: Just walk about.

Barry: I can't stand just like walking around all day and doing nothing when I could be, I don't know, pissed or something.

Alex: As long as you've got money you can do something; but if you've got no money, then ...

Shelley: You can still sort things out.

Barry: Bollocks.

Shelley: You can look for a job and that.

Barry: Oh yeah [sarcastic]. You can do that, yeah.

Alex: Doss round even more; get stoned even more. That's about it.

Barry: Sit on the wall outside [the hostel]; talk; mess about. Then we get let back in here and have something to eat and watch the telly.

Those looking to spend the day 'dossing round town' usually head for the high street and shopping centre. The high street is lined with a busy medley of shoe shops, department stores, sportswear outlets, jewellers stores and newspaper kiosks, and those with only time to spend can at any rate browse and window shop here. The myriad pedestrians jostling past one another, eyeing their plate-glass reflections and struggling to manoeuvre pushchairs through shop doorways also provide ample opportunity for people-watching. With even a little money to spend, say 50p, one can at least slip into a café and linger over a cup of tea for a good hour until asked to move on; £5 is plenty and will buy cigarettes, a magazine, a can of drink and crisps and a trip to the games arcade. The latter is a popular haunt – a sure place to meet friends, it also offers plenty by way of distraction and spectacle and holds out (to those who can afford to play) the possibility of briefly excelling at the pool table or the video game console. The shopping centre is a modern development housing a range of stores, most of them a little more upmarket than those on the high street. The decor is much the same as can be found in shopping centres throughout Britain: tiled walkways and chrome and glass balconies linked by escalators; larger concourses dotted with fixed benches and greenery; piped music and security guards. The shopping centre is generally preferred to the high street – the shops are more fash-ionable and interesting, the layout is more varied, the benches provide a convenient place to gather and pass comment on the bustle of consumers, and it is always dry and warm.[5]

Walking around all day is no fun on your own, but you do not have to walk around for long before bumping into others at a similarly loose end. For the most part residents, ex-residents and friends hang out together in town in small gangs – talking, smoking cigarettes, messing about and waiting for something to happen. Although they are rarely doing all that much (and for just that reason sometimes) they are a conspicuous presence in the town centre and undesirable in the eyes of many shop

5. Commenting on young people's occupation of Britain's town centres, Paul Willis writes: '[t]he busiest concourses of human activity and movement, the main focus for all those warm bodies doing things and supplying endless possibilities for observation, humour and interaction is, of course, the shopping centre ... what more natural for groups of kids to be attracted to these bright and active places – and what better sites either for the longings of a frustrated consumerism – or for mischief to, challenge and exposure of those trapped in it. Perhaps both at once' (1984a: 21).

owners. Groups 'loitering' outside stores are often asked to move
on; friends thumbing through clothes rails or CD racks with little
intention to buy are watched closely by store detectives and
made to feel unwelcome. If a group of young people are making
a show of themselves and behaving a little too boisterously in
the high street then the police may take an interest and move
them on – although those who have nowhere else to go will soon
drift back. The shopping centre is the most contested space.
Private security guards patrol here constantly and make it their
business to keep gangs of idle young people to a minimum,
physically removing any individuals whom they consider to be
a disruption.

In good weather the park provides an alternative venue,
somewhere to laze and loaf unharassed; but there is less here to
see and do than in and around the town centre.

Not all those who are out of doors during the day are simply
killing time. Some will be pounding the streets between the DSS,
the JobCentre and the Careers Service, trying to sort whatever it
is that has gone awry with their benefits this time. Others will
have equally pressing matters to attend to – a 'no more excuses'
appointment with their probation officer perhaps. With a
hospital check-up to get to in the morning, a midday meeting
with her social worker and plans to visit her boyfriend in prison
in the afternoon, Suzie is rushed off her feet, not kicking her
heels.

Evenings are a slightly different proposition. The high street
stores and the DSS and other offices are all closed, the shopping
centre is locked up and the streets are generally quieter.
Southerton's nightlife, such as it is, is off-limits to those like
Cherie or Alan who have only just turned 16. Those old enough
to get served in the town's bars and pubs, or who look old
enough, are usually happier drinking cans of lager together on
the benches in the park or back at someone's bedsit. Cannabis is
much more popular, and cheaper, than alcohol served at pub
prices. The Starburst, one of a handful of local nightclubs, targets
the teenage market; but it is even more expensive than the local
pubs. An evening spent on the dance floor can only be a very
occasional event, once a month perhaps, a night out to look
forward to and to be remembered afterwards, not something to
do in-between-times. There is no local youth club. A sports centre

and a leisure complex, with cinema and bowling alley, are a long walk or a short bus ride away, but the cost is, again, prohibitive. Yet most evenings ex-residents drift down to Lime Street in twos and threes to drink a cup of coffee and see if anyone feels like coming out for a few hours – to wander into town or to mess about outside the hostel discussing the day's events. Evenings spent out of doors have an edge that is not there in the daytime, even if very little actually happens. For those who have only recently left home and school there is still something new and exciting about time spent together on the streets at night when others are safely indoors.

Come 11 o' clock those staying at the hostel must head back to Lime Street in time for lights out. Others with a place of their own may stay out a little longer, lingering outside the kebab shop to see if there is any trouble as the pubs close, before making their way home to bed or to watch television for a few hours. Those with nowhere to go – one or two, perhaps, who have been casual enough to have left things this late – will be casting around now for a favour, looking to tag along back to someone's room and spend a night on the sofa or the floor.

Trouble

Young people who have moved on from the hostel and want to stay out of trouble stop indoors and do not keep company, but this is hard, hard work. Time spent outside and in a crowd, away from the bedsits and the hostel, is less predictable. The streets hold out the possibility at least that something new and unexpected will happen.

Of course, on the slowest days there is precious little to do, outside or in. Sitting on the bonnet of a car parked outside the hostel, Shane is simply

> ... bored. When this place [the hostel] is closed I want to get in, but when it's open I want to go out.

All the same, hanging around on street corners and in the town centre it is action and incident – trouble – that young people like Shane are looking for, and they have more chance of finding it out in the open than they do behind closed doors.

Sometimes they are no more than spectators, chasing events across town as word spreads that there has been a police raid on a house on Marlborough Hill or some incident in the high street. On other occasions trouble comes to them. Groups of young people in the town centre find themselves brought to the attention of the authorities even (and perhaps especially) when they are not doing anything in particular. With little or no money to spend and nothing much to do, Billy, Jono and Jack look a little out of place in the shopping centre, and for this reason alone they can find themselves in conflict with the security guards. This may seem grossly unfair, and certainly these three will protest their innocence when asked to leave the centre on a rainy afternoon; but they are not always as artless in this as they claim to be. Sometimes the attention of the centre security guards is mischievously invited, just to see what will happen. With an hour to go until the hostel opens for the evening, residents fed up with walking around town will lounge on the benches in the shopping centre concourse, acting up and trying it on with the guards, groups of onlookers jeering and cheering as one of their number is escorted out, and then melting away before the guards return. This sort of fooling around and rowdy behaviour may be no more than a nuisance much of the time, but occasionally these confrontations get out of hand. Both Al and Danny have appeared in court as a result of ill-tempered clashes with the security guards.

When high spirits shade off into overtly anti-social behaviour the results are predictable. Marky is always mouthing off under his breath at the police, but when he throws stones at a passing police van he can hardly be surprised to find himself arrested and on his way to the police station. Similarly, when Scott gets drunk and starts shouting at passers-by on the high street it does not take long for the police to intervene.

It is not at all unusual for the police to ring the hostel with the news that a resident has been arrested following some or other incident in the town centre. Shoplifting is a common charge. The shop owners and store detectives who mistrustfully monitor teenagers in the town centre stores are not acting entirely on idle suspicion – the majority of the young people who pass through the Lime Street hostel have stolen from the local shops at one time or another. The family row that first brought Tara to Lime

Street started out as a talking-to from her father about shoplifting (a police officer had brought her home to face the music after she had been caught stealing cosmetics from the chemist). For most residents at the hostel, shoplifting is an occasional dare. Egging each other on in the high street, they are looking for ways in which to liven up an otherwise uneventful afternoon. As a general rule it is the younger residents who pilfer from the shops the most. Alan is one such, a prolific shoplifter. He regularly brings bags of brand-new CDs back to the hostel in late afternoon, leaving the staff team wondering how best to confront him about this. Those who have moved on from Lime Street also raid the high street stores from time to time for inessential bits and pieces for their rooms, things that they see every day in the shop windows and cannot afford to buy; they are also more likely to steal simply to make ends meet, making an occasional foray to the corner shop for coffee and milk and biscuits whenever their giro runs out. Vicky regularly supplements her social security income by shoplifting for groceries at the supermarket on Stanley Street.

Some of those who are out of doors in the evenings also dabble in petty, opportunistic crime – climbing over fences into private gardens looking for mountain bikes to steal, trying the doorhandles of parked cars. And again, these activities are as much about running the risk as they are about securing any material gain.

Craig: Did you hear about me and Bagsy doing the smash and grab one night? Me and Bagsy sneaked out [of the hostel] one night ... all dressed in black – totally. We sneaked up to a shop and tried smashing the window with a brick, but we got nowhere. It just bounced off the window and the alarm went off and we legged it and sat in the park and had a cigarette. We thought 'We can't go back with nothing' so Bagsy nicked a shirt off a washing line. We walked round people's back gardens for a while thinking 'What shall we nick?' but we couldn't think of nothing so we went back to the hostel.

Craig and Bagsy did not get into any trouble over this particular late night venture, but both have criminal records. A majority of the young people coming to stay on Lime Street have been in trouble with the police at one time or another, of which there is a smaller number, a minority, whose criminal activity is substantial and who are busy building up sizeable criminal records.

*   *   *

Roy and Tony turn up at my bedsit, both of them a little high, just calling in out of curiosity. I make coffee and Roy paces up and down, talking non-stop about what he has been up to.

'Where's Trev man? I don't know where he's gone, he's disappeared. We was supposed to meet him tonight ... we was supposed to be going and earning some money. Guess how much I spent today man, right? I had £100 this morning and all I've got left now is £15, and I haven't even bought any food and that. I've got my old trainers back now. Those black and white ones were doing my head in. Anyway, I can run faster in these. Yeah man ... we got arrested the other night – thirteen hours in a police cell, and I ain't getting charged mate. Tony is though. I've been in and out of police cells all week, it's doing my head in. Me and Trev told Tony the other night to come on out on the rob and do a few cars with us ... we weren't even down the road from Tony's house and the next car to come round the corner was the police. Man, unlucky or what? He says, 'Oi, come here you two little bastards!' You should see him trying to get the cuffs on Tony – he couldn't do it ... I'm getting £173 off of the social services. I will, yeah. How much you want to bet? I've had loads of money off them cos they're still supposed to be in charge of me. I'm still supposed to be in school, that's why, I think. I haven't been to school for ages man ... I'd rather be outside. You know those snap-on tool sets? I've had loads of those. That's what we had last night, that's what Tony got nicked for. I've got to pay my fines tomorrow. Can I borrow 20p? Can I borrow £1? ... Oh yeah I forgot about your torch, but that wasn't my fault man. I left that in school man. We broke into school and I dropped it in a puddle cos we had to run. We had to climb over a boiler cos that's how we got in man, yeah. You know —— [the local supermarket], well they've got loads of cash in there man. Loads of it. I've seen it in that office. Serious stuff. I wouldn't mind getting caught for £3,000, as long as I had it stashed away somewhere.'

Suddenly bored, Roy decides to head off to look for his friend Trev. Tony stays to finish his coffee.

*   *   *

Roy is a tabloid editor's dream: a 16-year-old who should still be attending school, but who is breaking into it instead, for whom crime is a source of excitement but also, it would appear, a means of 'earning' considerable amounts of money (an income which nonetheless slips through his fingers so fast that he can't even account for it at the end of the day), who has spent 'all week' in the police station, but is confident of not getting caught again (and is sure that, if he does, he will be able to wriggle out of it somehow or get off lightly), and who is daydreaming about the kind of crime that could land him in prison for a number of years. But Roy's criminal activity is prodigious only in aggregate; considered incident by incident his offending is (thus far) small-scale: he is a petty thief, stealing opportunistically from cars and shops and occasionally breaking into unoccupied buildings at night to see what takes his fancy.

Roy is homeless, and this has a good deal to do with why he steals. Having left the hostel and quit his room on Victoria Road, and with his benefits in disarray, he relies on theft and shoplifting to generate an erratic and occasionally substantial income. With money to spend, and bearing gifts, he is not short of offers from friends with a space on their floor. Crime provides an occasional, alternative source of cash for those who fall foul of the DSS, but in practice the proceeds rarely amount to all that much. Certainly no one makes anything like a living out of it for any length of time, not even Roy. And the bottom line is that those who do go out 'on the rob' are always getting caught. As a result, they are often, seemingly inextricably, entangled in the criminal justice system. Michael, another sometime resident on Lime Street, and a year older than Roy, must report to the police station every day as a condition of his bail and is on a night-time curfew that keeps him indoors after 9.00 p.m.; he is due to appear in court again in a few weeks' time, but is reoffending quicker than the legal system can keep up; he has appointments to keep with both his youth justice worker and his solicitor later this week, and is still paying fines dating from his last appearance in front of the magistrates.

The exploits of young offenders like Roy and Michael provide a vicarious excitement for others who are not so often in trouble. When the police call at the hostel to make an arrest, residents crowd around the stairs in the hallway to watch what happens and will later walk over to the police station to wait outside for news of any further developments. Similarly, the public gallery of the local magistrates court is often cluttered with groups of Lime Street residents past and present who have turned up to show support for friends and spectate.

*   *   *

Having spent last night in the cells, Stephen is due to appear in court this morning. The story of his arrest has spread quickly from the hostel through the bedsits, and various friends are headed into town to watch the proceedings.

Since coming to Lime Street a few weeks ago, referred by his probation officer, Stephen has cultivated a hard-boiled, savvy persona. At 19 years old, he is one of the more senior residents and has been spending time away from the hostel, hanging out with Raymond at his bedsit on Springfield Avenue. Raymond is older too and, like Stephen, has spent some years in and out of housing difficulties; both young men have spent time in prison. Yesterday morning, Stephen let it be known that he was off into London to see some 'serious people' about money owing to him for a 'job' he did before he went 'inside'. No one saw him all day until he showed up at the hostel in the early evening, banging on the door, the sleeve of his jacket soaked in blood, claiming to have been stabbed. One of the characters he was supposed to meet pulled a knife on him and there had been some sort of struggle, at the end of which Stephen ran off leaving his assailant on the floor, possibly dead.

The police called at the hostel five minutes after Stephen's dramatic appearance and arrested him.

The hostel and the bedsits have been alive with talk about this incident, and as we walk over to the court buildings – Adrian, Tara, myself and half a dozen others – there is a lot of wild speculation about the charges Stephen will face. It is clear that there will be a large audience in court. But once proceedings are under way, a rather different account of yesterday's events begins to emerge. It seems Stephen spent most of the day drinking with his cousin, and then made a clumsy attempt to steal more beer from an off-licence, got into a fight with the proprietor, and accidentally swung his arm through a glass counter. His sensational, heroic tale of yesterday is reduced to a much more banal story of shoplifting and drunken brawling. He is remanded in custody and led away.[6] Filing out of the building, Adrian and Tara hint darkly that, luckily for Stephen, the police have not found out what really went on – but we all know that this is not true.

*   *   *

For all that they provide a welcome diversion, court appearances are often something of an anticlimax for those in the public gallery. After a lot of waiting around, a catalogue of bungled and petty crimes, stripped of elaboration and exaggeration, is worked through briskly and with little fuss or drama.[7] Those who have upcoming court cases may be cocky in the weeks leading up to their big day, affecting an insouciance as to what may happen to them, but this bravado invariably dwindles and on the day they usually cut rather anxious, timid figures. Almost all are advised, and agree, to plead guilty, and the eventual outcome, at the end of what may be a series of appearances and adjournments drawn out over several months, is usually some combination of supervision, community work and fines; prison sentences are rare, but are a possibility for (usually older) persistent offenders.[8]

Stephen is one of only a few young men coming to stay on Lime Street – about one in every ten – who have criminal

6. Any young person appearing in court with no fixed abode is likely to be refused bail unless some arrangement can be made there and then; and, in what can prove a vicious circle for some young people, time spent in custody on remand is linked in turn to the risk of homelessness on release (see Thornton, 1990: 22–3). The magistrates' judgment in Stephen's case is that he is likely to reoffend if released on bail, not least because, as a resident at the hostel, he will be on the streets and at a loose end most weekday afternoons.

7. Stephen's 15 minutes of fame proves more of a damp squib than most, given his rather incredible tale of derring-do of the evening before – which is not to make light of the considerable alarm and distress he doubtless caused the poor newsagent.

8. Far fewer of the young women coming to stay on Lime Street ever appear in court or get in trouble with the police for anything other than occasional shoplifting or possession of drugs. It is Suzie who visits her boyfriend on remand, and Tara who is in court to see what happens to Stephen, not the other way around. This does not prevent female residents at the hostel, and those in the bedsits, getting into various kinds of trouble as a result of the illegal activities of their male friends and associates (as happens to Cherie on Marlborough Hill (see pages 74–5).

convictions for violent offences such as ABH (actual bodily harm), GBH (grievous bodily harm) and affray, or are due to appear in court to face such charges. But many more besides, an overwhelming majority, have been involved in fights and scuffles on the streets of Southerton, some of them quite brutal, that have never come before the courts. Al's black eye (see page 81) is a memento of one such incident.

*   *   *

Al has been in a fight. Jono brings him round to my bedsit to get him cleaned up. Al is worried that he can see nothing out of his right eye, and we end up taking him to the hospital. On the way there, Jono tells me what happened.

'We were just coming back from the hostel, through the park, when they stopped us. I was standing quite a bit back and this guy, Kirk, was arguing with Al and then he grabs him by his hair and starts smacking his head on the floor. I didn't start anything cos there was more of them. Then, when they were walking off, one of them head-butted me. But I just laughed at them, cos I know Kirk and he knows my brother, so he wouldn't touch me or my brother would kill him.'

*   *   *

Like most fights, Al and Kirk's set-to was the product of a long-standing feud, one of the many such feuds that circulate around the bedsit grapevine until they either blow over or end in some physical confrontation. This one could have gone either way, until the chance encounter in the park forced the issue.

Al did not go out looking for a fight – this sort of trouble is rarely sought out – but he did not back down from it either. He would rather not have been on the receiving end, but in having stood his ground he has at least saved face. Next time it may be his turn to catch his assailant outnumbered. Violence and intimidation are miserable things; the fights and brawls that the young people passing through Lime Street get into are usually bewildering and frightening occasions for all those involved – win or lose. But the ability to look after oneself, to take what comes, come what may, is at stake here. And it follows that, as with tales of criminal exploits, stories told about fights are prone to exaggeration. The day after it has happened, a fight can be almost unrecognisable in the retelling. Narrators and audience quickly collude in constructing coherent tests of character out of what, at the time, were vicious and often inconclusive events. Scott's account of a fight he had with a young man called Martin sounds more like a scene from a Western when he tells it several weeks after the event.

> *Scott*: Me and Martin had a disagreement and we went out to the car park and had a fight. And I was, like, running round him in circles: bang, bang, bang [jabs punches in the air to demonstrate]. And then he grabbed me and goes donk, donk [grabs himself round the neck and wallops his own head]; and I go flop [collapses], out cold. And then, the next minute, I was on my feet: bang, bang, bang. And then he'd grab me: donk; flop. And I jump up again. About six times he knocked me out. But in the end, after about half an hour, I done him. I fucking slaughtered him. But I felt such a cunt afterwards I pulled him up and we went for a drink together.

If he is fooling anyone at all with this imaginative account, Scott is fooling himself. It can, of course, be nice to be fooled; and there are plenty at the hostel and in the bedsits ready to listen to stories like this. Scott needs to hear it too – a reassuringly knockabout reworking of an unpleasant experience.

Fights not only settle scores (and, in truth, they rarely do this once and for all), they have a part to play in the making and breaking of local reputations – establishing who is 'hard' and who is not, who can stand up for themselves and who can be pushed around. There are other factors at work here too. Roy is physically slight – still only a boy – but he is well-connected and respected accordingly. Colin is from out of town and an unknown quantity; he has a quiet charisma and authority that no one has felt inclined to test thus far. Raymond has been around and has spent time 'inside', but at 22 years old he is not so much a player in this game as he once was. Most of the young people hanging out on Southerton's streets are implicated one way or another in an intricate web of respective judgement and estimation. Residents at the hostel and those in the bedsits 'know about' many more local young people than they actually know, those whose reputations precede them.

Richie: You hear about a lot of people. I've heard about this geezer called Davy, right, from different people – that he's a nutter, a head-case and everything. But he was at court yesterday ... [and we got talking] ... and, like, the way we were speaking, I wouldn't personally take him as hard as everyone says. You know what I mean? Cos he seems a sound geezer. He said he's heard of me, and I've heard of him. That's what happens.

Word of mouth reputations of this sort are precious, certainly so for those who feel they have little else to show for themselves. Many of the younger arrivals on Lime Street are keen to make a name for themselves locally; but this can be a difficult, and delicate, undertaking, to be worked at carefully. Those who are over-eager and make rather too much of themselves risk being taught a lesson and taken down a peg or two; those who have the weight to throw around must do so judiciously, or they will be treated with due deference only until their back is turned. There is a continual jostling for position among the young people out and about on the streets during the afternoons and evenings. Threatening stares and gestures are exchanged whenever groups of young people run across one another outside the games arcade or in the shopping centre; and although this sort of posturing usually stops short of physical confrontation, there is always the possibility that someone's bluff will be called and a fight will ensue.[9]

There is a measure of excitement to be had from this – the buzz of rumour about who is out to get who, and the dramatic tension as groups and individuals size one another up in the high street – but for those on the receiving end of threats and intimidation the anxiety can be wearing.

*   *   *

Tara hears from a friend that Chantelle is out to get her for something – she doesn't know what; the news has put her on edge and she is angry and upset. She walks down from her bedsit to Lime Street to

9. The girls and young women passing through Lime Street do not compete with one another on quite the same terms as the boys and young men do, but they have reputations to protect and foster too, by force if it comes to that. Vicky, Tara, Cherie and Yvonne have all been involved in fights with rivals in the town centre.

speak to Marky, hoping that he can explain, as he knows Chantelle and used to go out with her. In the middle of their conversation, Marky is called outside to speak to Sean and Frazier. Marky owes money to Sean, and, with Frazier standing by toying with a sharpened screwdriver, he feels he has little choice but to pay up. He fetches his order book and signs over his next week's giro to Sean.[10] Coming back into the front room, his hands are shaking.

'Fucking Southerton. It's always "You're going to get it", or "He's going to get it", or "She's going to get it." It drives you mad. I tell you, I've had enough of it Tom. I'm just going to buy a tent and go – anywhere, so long as it's out of this shit-hole.'

* * *

The threats and intimidation that Marky complains about are internecine and juvenile, and no less real and vicious for that; but violence can come from adults as well as from peers. There are almost always young people at the hostel who have left family and domestic violence of some sort behind them; Bagsy bears a vivid scar on his arm as a memento of his time sleeping rough in London; Aimee returns to Lime Street for a second stay when she is attacked by a stranger in her (poorly secured) bedsit room. And there are even a few local landlords who are prepared to come down hard on young tenants who get out of hand.

* * *

Adrian, evicted from his bedsit room and living at the hostel, is soon to be a father. His pregnant girlfriend, Louise, lives on Victoria Road, at Number 55, in a tiny bedsit room. The two of them hope to secure a council flat before the baby arrives, but in the meantime things are difficult – Adrian cannot visit Louise as he has been banned from the property by the landlord, who has received complaints from the neighbours about noisy, late-night arguments. (Adrian and Louise's landlord have a difficult history, dating back to when Adrian was a tenant on Victoria Road himself.)

10. Those who are unable to work and whose claim is likely to last for a few months are usually paid by order book, rather than by a fortnightly giro sent by post (see Child Poverty Action Group, 2002). Marky is 'on the sick': long-term illness is keeping him out of the job market.

Having spent a few hours at the hostel one evening, Louise asks Adrian to walk her home; the two of them leave the hostel with Ben, another resident. Minutes later Ben is back, out of breath, demanding that Poppy phone the police: a fight has broken out between Adrian, Louise's landlord and another man. Adrian returns a few minutes later, bloodied and visibly shaking.

'I've just had the shit beaten out of me', he shouts, searching in his bag for a length of pipe he keeps there for emergencies.

Poppy tries to get more details, telling Adrian to stay put while she phones the police. It seems that Adrian and Louise went indoors together only to find the landlord and his son in the hallway, collecting rent. An argument broke out, punches were thrown and Adrian was forced out onto the street and then set upon when he tried to get back inside to check that Louise was unhurt.

Louise arrives back at the hostel, sobbing, mascara running down her face; the police are close behind. Adrian is too angry and incoherent to make a statement, and so the matter is left until the morning. A policewoman escorts Louise back to her bedsit.

*   *   *

When Adrian reaches in his bag for a length of pipe he is close to an escalation of violence that could end terribly, and he is not the only one to come this close. Richie, Bagsy, Scott, Craig, Danny and several others all carry knives on their person when out on the streets sometimes; a few do so as a matter of course, reasoning that a knife is a deterrent rather than a liability or provocation – a signal to others that there is to be no trouble.[11] Thus, brandishing a sharpened screwdriver, Frazier turns the confrontation with Marky (see page 95) into a set piece, in which Marky has no choice but to pay up. But there are myriad other more explosive encounters – Al's run-in with Kirk, for one (see page 92) – where a knife, carried on a whim perhaps and for no more than the secret thrill of it, might easily change things for ever. As Scott acknowledges:

Scott: The problem with carrying a knife is that one day you'll use it.

11. New arrivals at the hostel are routinely asked to hand over any weapons in their possession – a locked drawer in the staff office holds a clutter of Stanley knives and switchblades.

Many more skate across this thin ice than fall through it – which is something to be thankful for; but some do fall through all the same.

*   *   *

Shane calls round to the hostel for the first time in a couple of months – he has been living in a bedsit a few miles out of town. He stays at the hostel for most of the evening and asks if he can sleep over, but is told no. When the staff lock up for the night he wanders around the town centre for a few hours and, more out of boredom than anything else, breaks into a local newsagent's shop. A couple of days later he is back at the hostel again, with the news that he has been evicted from his bedsit for stealing the live-in landlord's television. He is booked in for his second stay on Lime Street.

A week into his stay, Shane disappears without explanation. After two days absence, his name is taken off the list of residents on the board in the staff office and his bed is given to a young man referred to the hostel by the ABC project. That evening, the staff get a phone call from a police station in central London: Shane is in the cells for the night, dead drunk. The following day he is back on Lime Street, fed up to find that his bed has been taken and angry at himself for messing things up. The staff contact his social worker, but finding Shane somewhere else to stay proves very difficult. Social services have only one place available on their emergency lodgings scheme, and they admit that it is not ideal. Shane refuses to go there.

'Not that old lady with the fucking cats. I've been there before, she drove me fucking mad. I won't stay there.'

Ann agrees to house him for one more night. As the hostel is full, he sleeps on the sofa in the front room.

Shane spends the whole of the next day going back and forth between Lime Street, the ABC project and the social services department. By the end of the afternoon he is no further on: he still has nowhere to stay. That evening the police call at the hostel to speak to him about the break-in at the newsagent's shop. Shane confesses and spends the night in custody.

Having appeared in court the next morning, Shane goes to meet his social worker, who is still trying to find him somewhere to stay. As a result, he misses an appointment at the Careers Service. He has no idea where he will be sleeping that night and has run out of money, with no giro due for another week. He is extremely discouraged and on edge.

'What a head-fuck of a day. This is doing my fucking head in. I feel like my head's going to explode. Honestly, my head feels like a fucking volcano ... I think I'm just going to leave. I'm going to Manchester. Fuck it.'

He borrows some money from Ann and goes out to get cigarettes. When he returns he is drunk and in an angry mood; he has been involved in a confrontation between a group of residents and a local teenage gang, in the town centre. He takes a cook's knife from the kitchen and marches towards the front door. Poppy tells him that if he leaves the hostel with the knife she will call the police. Shane ignores her.

Ten minutes later, in the centre of town, the situation has got out of hand. Four police cars and two police vans are blocking the high street; one of the vans is pulled across a shop doorway, where Shane is brandishing the knife at six police officers gathered either side of him – he is threatening to stab anyone who comes near him. Marky has already been arrested and is lying across the bonnet of a police car with his hands cuffed behind him. Cherie is there too, among a gathering crowd of onlookers, trying to persuade Shane to put the knife down. Eventually a police officer in body armour enters the doorway and knocks the knife out of Shane's hand. Shane is handcuffed, tossed into one of the vans and taken to the police station. In court, the next morning, he is remanded to a young people's secure unit.

*   *   *

Shane's six-month odyssey since leaving home has comprised two stays at the hostel, a month in Al's bedsit, a few weeks spent stringing together stop-gap living arrangements, a handful of nights out of doors, a short-lived tenancy in a room of his own and a miscarried jaunt into London. In this time he has become a familiar face around town, a regular at the games arcade and one of the same crowd of hangers-on and visitors at Vicky and Jones' place on Stanley Street and other properties on Victoria Road and Marlborough Hill. He is well-known to the local police, the security guards in the shopping centre – from which he is banned – the workers at the DSS and Careers Service and the staff at both the ABC project and the Lime Street hostel.

Now that he has reached the end of some sort of line and is out of circulation, the scant possessions he left at the hostel will be packed away and stacked with other cardboard boxes full of the abandoned belongings of previous residents. His dramatic exit will provide a talking point for days and perhaps weeks – at the hostel, in the bedsits, on the high street; and it may be that repercussions and further confrontations will follow. Some of those who knew Shane only in passing may claim a closer acquaintance now that he is gone, looking to enhance their own reputations. Others will have been given pause for thought, and, relieved that they were not caught up in things on this occasion, will wonder if it might be time to review their own situation and maybe 'slow down' a little (see Samantha's comments on page 54). The hostel staff will talk things over at the next staff meeting, but they will not dwell too long on Shane's problems, now that he is no longer their responsibility. They have learned to take events like this in their stride. As has Raymond, who is unsurprised but sympathetic, seeing in Shane something of himself only a few years ago.

Raymond: I could see that coming – Shane was always going to do some time. But hard times build character, they say.

Exactly what it is that hard times build, if they really build all that much at all, is the focus of the next chapter.

5
Growing Apart?

The young homeless who come and go from Lime Street are down but not out – at least not yet.

That things are difficult for them is not in question. They are away from home and parents, and their housing situation – moving between emergency accommodation, rented bedsit rooms and other, stop-gap living arrangements – is precarious. Some do not settle anywhere for more than a couple of months, and return, repeatedly, to the Lime Street hostel. Most are without work, or, at best, have some little experience of low-paid, part-time or temporary employment; many are only just past school-leaving age. They get by, most of them (and some better than others), on the periphery of the welfare system. Some slip through the benefits net entirely from time to time and make do without any visible means of support. For the most part they endure the inevitable boredom and frustrations of life on the margins: spending hours sitting watching television in the front room at the hostel; passing time in the confinement of cheap bedsit rooms; hanging out together, doing nothing, in the town centre. This monotony is intermittently punctuated by recurrent dramas, upheavals and personal misadventures. Some days do not so much drag as fly by, in a flurry of activity, as individuals scramble to deal with whatever turmoil they have walked into or had visited upon them. These ups and downs make for a bumpy psychological ride through extremes of depression, enthusiasm, anger and exhaustion. For those who have been in the bedsits long enough however, even the most frantic days can come to seem static somehow – in the very midst of whatever crisis they are coping with they will sometimes confess to a desperate sense of having been here before, of the days going nowhere.

This is not a rosy picture, but those passing through the Lime Street hostel have not, by any means, reached the end of the line. They are, in many ways, only just setting out in life. Where, then, are they headed, and what will become of them? This question, writ large, was asked time and again during the 1990s, amidst a swell of public disquiet about the numbers of young people in Britain who were visibly losing out. The disquiet was twofold. Alongside an immediate concern for those struggling through hard times there was a wary anxiety that hard times could be building something other than character. It was in this context that the term 'underclass' entered the contemporary social problems vocabulary.

Finding Fault

What is an underclass? Ralf Dahrendorf suggests that, in everyday language at least, it makes an obvious sort of sense 'to talk about people in human societies who are not able, or perhaps willing, or both, to participate fully in the economic, the political and the social life of the communities in which they are living' (1992: 55), but it has been on precisely this point – not able, or perhaps willing, or both – that speculation about a burgeoning British underclass has turned. For the most part, and despite fierce objections (see Lister, 1996), it has been the idea that there are those at the margins not willing to make the effort to regain the social mainstream to which the word underclass has given expression.

In the first of his two contributions to the British underclass debate, Charles Murray sketched out a list of social problems, which, in combination and on the rise, were, he argued, symptomatic of an emergent underclass – '[d]rugs, crime, illegitimacy, homelessness, drop out from the job market, drop out from school, casual violence' (1990: 2). There is nothing here that is outside the common experience of those coming to stay at the Lime Street hostel. Richie's potted life-history (see pages 21–2) might be made-to-measure as an illustration of the sort of lifestyle that Murray is writing about. And the resemblance is more than passing. Many of Southerton's young homeless seem to act in ways which lend support to the interpretive take that Murray favours, implicating themselves (wittingly or not) in the perpetuation of their own straitened circumstances, not least their precarious housing situation. A significant number of those leaving Lime Street to move into rented rooms are back at the hostel before too long, homeless again. Some of these young people could be described as intentionally homeless; certainly those who have walked out on their accommodation, but also many of those who have been evicted. As Oscar Wilde might have put it: to lose one's accommodation once may be regarded as a misfortune; to lose it twice or three times in as many months looks like carelessness. And there are others, who do not return to the hostel but who can hardly be described as settled in their accommodation; those who continue to drift between rooms, occasionally falling back on stop-gap living arrangements as if they were not that inclined to take housing and the risk of further homelessness all that seriously. Then there is the question of work and benefits. The young people coming to Lime Street are, almost all of them, unemployed; and the majority remain so when they leave, living on a social security income, their rent paid through housing benefit. The residents at the hostel aside, those in the bedsits (their housing problems resolved for the moment) ought surely to be looking for work; and yet, for all the time that they have on their hands, they could hardly be described as avid job-seekers. Nor are they all that dutiful and 'deserving' as claimants of social security (see Howe, 1985; and Cullen and Howe, 1991). In their dealings with the DSS they come across as pushy and deceitful at times, or else too lazy or careless to keep their claims in order. And the local police know some of these young people only too well – those who make a public nuisance of themselves in the town centre, and that handful of repeat offenders whose burgeoning criminal records not only compound their present difficulties, but will undoubtedly damage their longer-term prospects.

Given full rein, these arguments reach a familiar conclusion: the young homeless should take some responsibility for their situation, settle for whatever they can find by way of accommodation (or go back home to their parents), do their best to get themselves off the dole and into work, and stay out of trouble in the meantime. Any who choose not to take these steps have only themselves to blame, and must forfeit public sympathy and support.

But this is not the only conclusion to be drawn from the preceding chapters. It should also be clear that the young homeless coming to Lime Street are in a tight corner, and that the lives they are leading are hedged in by circumstances that they are poorly positioned to do all that much about. And a causal analysis that starts out from and stays close to this baseline – the material constraints that the young homeless are up against – is likely to arrive at a different judgement, one in which no one chooses to be homeless (Evans, 1996).

Housing, its availability and quality, must surely count for something in any account of homelessness in Southerton, or anywhere else for that matter; and the inescapable truth is that the young people coming and going from Lime Street have very limited housing options. They are not in any position to consider owner occupation, they have no significant access to public (council) housing and are priced out of the bulk of the private rented market. This leaves them looking to meet their housing needs at the very tail end of the private rented sector, where conditions are generally poor and the rooms leave a lot to be desired. Furthermore, and crucially, those moving from Lime Street into the bedsits must manage on only a minimum income, juggling whatever debts they are already carrying, and without the diverse, ongoing support – financial, practical and emotional – of parents and family.[1] Home alone, some of them for the very first time and perhaps a year or two sooner than they would otherwise have chosen, it should come as no surprise that they struggle to make a go of things.

So far as jobs go, the situation is much the same. The greater part of the local labour market is effectively off-limits to teenage hopefuls with little work experience and few qualifications. This is why so many of those leaving the hostel are on the dole. The situation is not entirely hopeless; there is work to be had for some if not all, but only in part-time and temporary jobs that are not all that appealing or rewarding. Staff turnover at this end of the labour market is high; few employees stay for long, or are expected to. Most of those in the bedsits get by on benefits, and getting by is just about all that such an income allows; the

1. For the majority of young people in Britain today, the process of leaving home is a drawn-out one. Many remain, to some degree, financially dependent on their parents for some time after they have left home, and may return to live with them on subsequent occasions, or at least draw some comfort (and security) from the knowledge that there is a room waiting for them in the family home should they need it (see Jones and Wallace, 1992; Jones, 1995).

occasional boast about 'working the system' notwithstanding, there is little if any room for lucrative manoeuvre here. Life on the dole is harder still for those whose circumstances and accommodation remain unsettled; and many find that they have their work cut out just to keep their claims in order.[2] Any who fail to do so end up going days, and sometimes weeks, without any benefit income whatsoever. The likelihood of committing an offence is always going to be higher for young people living like this; much higher for those who inadvertently slip through the social security net.

In combination, this makes for a mutually reinforcing set of circumstances – unsettled housing and intermittent homelessness, continuing underemployment, repeated setbacks in claiming benefit and, for some, recurrent trouble with the police and a burgeoning criminal record – that it is hard to escape from or do all that much about, at least in the short term.

Which way to go, choice or constraint? Are the young homeless indifferent collaborators in their own exclusion, perhaps not that badly off after all and laughing up their sleeves at the rest of us? Or are they up against it and unable to do much about the predicament in which they find themselves?

Debate as to the causes of poverty and the character of the poor is evergreen. There is plenty of evidence to go round, enough to support both claim and counter-claim, and were there an easy, once-and-for-all answer we would have it by now. As it is, society will not let the matter drop; we worry at it constantly and will not accept any final adjudication. That this is so does not excuse any of us from making our own position clear, and I will make mine clear now, if it is not clear enough already: I spent over a year with a number of young homeless people, and

2. Consider the flux of circumstance that Yvonne experiences in the space of only six weeks (see pages 60–3). She signs off benefits, starts work, changes address, is laid off, signs on again, leaves her partner and changes address once more. Those for whom so much is up in the air do sometimes neglect and fall behind on their obligations as claimants, but not because they are lazy. They work hard at their claims. But their efforts come in fits and starts and are generally executed in arrears. Thus, Jones puts many more hours into being a claimant than most others on the dole in Southerton, but he does so because his claim is always getting snagged on some new turn of events, leaving him to rush down to the DSS to queue up, protest and plead his case.

so far as I could tell they were homeless neither because they wanted to be nor because they could not be bothered to do anything about it. This is a simple answer and none the worse for that, up to a point; but the question is, or ought to be, more complex to begin with. It does not help to make a zero sum game out of choice and constraint, such that only one or the other can prevail – *either* Cherie is careless about her accommodation *or* her room on Marlborough Hill falls a long way short of what she needs. The truth is that Cherie is careless about her accommodation *and* her room on Marlborough Hill falls a long way short of what she needs. Choice and constraint are both at work here, and not just alongside one another: they cross tracks and conjoin. Thus, and this is the crux of the matter, Cherie is careless about her accommodation *because* her room on Marlborough Hill falls a long way short of what she needs. And she is not the only one.

That Negative Crowd

A clockwork toy set running across the floor will sooner or later hit a wall, and when it does it will butt against the skirting board repeatedly, to no avail, until its spring winds down. People are different; not so bloody-minded or mechanical. Rather than push blindly on when the odds are stacked against us, we – all of us – make the best that we can of the circumstances in which we find ourselves. We cut our losses, conserve our energies, seize new and different opportunities as these present themselves; we come at things sideways when we see that coming at them straight on will do us no good. In short, we adjust and make do. And the young people passing through the hostel are no exception. They get by as best they can, bending their behaviour and expectations to fit the difficult circumstances in which they find themselves. This is not all that they do, but a good slice of life on Lime Street and Marlborough Hill and various stations in between is best understood on these terms.

Homeless off and on for six months, Max, like Cherie, has learned that bedsit rooms come and go and are not always worth holding on to; after an argument with his landlord he walks out of his room on Stanley Street, taking the contents of the hallway payphone with him, and moves in with Al. With her benefits finally sorted out after weeks of delay and wrangling, Jackie is not minded to start looking for work just yet – not until she has had a couple of giros, anyway. She spends her afternoons window shopping with Marcie, who is even less enthusiastic about spending time down the JobCentre:

> *Marcie*: It's a waste of time going there, anyway. There's no work, and even those jobs that are there are shit.

Settled at the same address on Victoria Road for three months, Jono is in the habit of staying in bed past noon – that way, he has less time to kill when he gets up, and a couple of bowls of cereal for 'breakfast' will generally see him all the way through to the evening. Three weeks behind on her bills and facing eviction, Tara spends half her fortnightly giro in a matter of hours on junk food, cigarettes, cannabis and cider. It hardly seems worth the effort trying to salvage anything from the mess she is in; and in any case, deep down, she would just as soon make the needle jump the groove as spend another two weeks on Catherine Street on £4.50 a day. One week on, not yet evicted and now broke, she is out and about 'on the scrounge' – borrowing money and shoplifting packets of soup from the supermarket.

Much of this and more besides, a whole hash of things said and done and let slide, makes sense enough *in situ*. If Max or Jackie or Tara are accessories to their own continuing difficulties this is not because they choose to be homeless or unemployed or whatever else, but because they are making what they can of the situation they are in. They are accessories after the fact, explanatory precedence resting with the difficulties they have been up against from the outset. Not that this puts any of them in any less of what Kevin calls 'a catch-22 situation'; nor is it difficult to see how lives led like this might coil these young people still further into their own predicament. There is little chance of Jono finding work lying in bed all morning, and six months down the line and no further on he will only be worse off, surely? The same goes for Max; the longer he spends ricocheting from one room to the next, the deeper the hole he is in. And as for Tara, who is to say that the provisional measures she is stringing together this week won't come to hand that much easier next week, perhaps settling into some sort of taken-for-granted pattern before too long: booze and drugs on giro day then a couple of weeks scrabbling around to make ends meet, running up favours and pilfering treats and staples from the shops; defaulting on the rent again; falling back on the hostel if and when the staff will have her back?

Tara may not have been away from home for all that much more than a couple of months, but there are others who have been kicking around Catherine Street and Marlborough Hill for a good while longer than this. On his own since leaving care two years ago, Joe arrives on Lime Street pretty much inured to the vagaries of teenage life on the dole at the bottom end of the housing market, and confident in his ability to roll with the punches:

> *Joe*: You've got to look after yourself haven't you? You know what I mean? That's just survival. You know what I'm saying mate? It's all out there mate ... and, round the corner, if things do go bang [i.e. take a turn for the worse], then ... [shrugs and turns his hands up in a gesture of indifference]. That's the way I look at it now; that's what it's done to me, I suppose. Now, instead of trying to prevent something from happening, [I look at it that] if it's going to happen, it happens. Simple as that, just be prepared for everything, that's the only thing it's taught me. Be prepared – for everything, [for] the worst.

Joe is experienced – 'a professional', Philip calls him; he knows his way around 'bedsit land' and the hostel circuit and has something of the measure of this life. He is one of those Kevin feels sure

> ... are just not going to change. It's too late for Joe, he's just not going to change, not now ... It comes from being in the streets and the different things that you go through; it becomes part of you and you can't change it – not unless you have a different type of setting.

How long, then, until Kevin is saying the same about Tara?

Joe is a disruptive presence on Lime Street: careless of the staff team's authority, and a little too sure of himself even for Ann's liking. The staff worry too that his breezy pessimism and swagger will rub off on the younger, impressionable residents; those like Leo, who left home only a week ago, arriving at the hostel just turned 16 years old and looking all of a nervous 12 or 13 at most.

> *Ann*: It's not good for Leo to stay here ... he's so vulnerable really, so easily led; he shouldn't be mixing with the Joes of this world.

Ann is keen to see Leo move back in with his parents. She feels it is 'too soon, way too soon' for him to be on his own in a bedsit somewhere; not least because, more likely than not, this will mean a bedsit on Marlborough Hill across the street from Marky, or upstairs from Tracy and Ed at Number 10 Victoria Road. This is not the sort of company she wants him to be keeping.

*   *   *

A month on from Cherie's exit from Marlborough Hill, her dad calls at the hostel to meet with Ann and Kevin. Cherie joins them in the staff office and they talk things through for over an hour – Cherie's relationship with her mum, the problems she had at school, the GCSEs she never sat, the mess she got into when she was living with Jim (see pages 15–16), the mess she got into when she was living with Tara (see pages 74–5), the money she has wasted on drugs. When Ann asks Cherie what it would take for her to settle somewhere next time, she launches into a roster of everything that went wrong with the room on Marlborough Hill; Dean and Tariq's names keep coming up.

Kevin suggests that Cherie might benefit from drugs counselling. Cherie is not so sure. But her dad backs the idea and tells her that if she signs up for a course, and attends all the sessions, he will pay the deposit on a flat for her.

'A nice little place, away from those others. Cos going back there [to Marlborough Hill] will do you no good girl, hanging out with all the druggies and divvies – cos that's what they are girl, fucking divvies. You need to get yourself sorted.'

The meeting over – Cherie now flopped out in the front room watching television and her dad gone home – Ann, Kevin and Poppy debrief over coffee. Ann does not want Dean and Tariq causing any more trouble for Cherie. 'She needs to stop seeing them if she's going to have any chance of not getting into more trouble than she's in already and getting her life sorted out ... she's going to have to keep away from them.'

Kevin agrees that these two are a poor influence. 'Their general attitude is, you know, the world owes me something and I'm going to get it any way I can.'

A decision is taken to bar Dean and Tariq from visiting the hostel. Seizing the moment, Kevin suggests that Jones is another who should be discouraged from stopping by. Not that Jones and Cherie are particularly close, but Jones is most definitely one of the 'druggie' crowd and his and Vicky's new place – they have moved on from Stanley

Street to a bedsit just around the corner from Lime Street – has fast become a focal point for residents looking to kill time on weekday afternoons. Jones has also been calling in at the hostel almost every evening of late, pestering the younger residents to lend him money.

'Cherie, Darren ... they need to straighten their lives out right now', says Kevin. 'And him coming by with that negative attitude – it's not helping them. And it's not helping us do our jobs.'

Ann and Poppy are persuaded: Jones is barred too.

A couple of days later, a Saturday morning, Richie rings the doorbell for the first time in almost two months. He is one ex-resident the staff have been hoping to hear from, and Ann invites him in for coffee and a chat. Richie tells Ann he is still living in the housing association property the staff helped him move to, but has been finding it hard on his own. The house is some distance out of town, and he has been feeling more than a little lonesome and bored; so bored, he says, that he has started looking for work. He pulls out an application form for a job at a supermarket, half completed.

'I got a City and Guilds in painting and decorating', he says, jabbing his finger at the form. 'But, like, my criminal record is quite big, isn't it? And people just look at it and don't want to give me a job. Experience? I ain't got none really, have I?'

Richie and I walk into town together. Standing outside the games arcade, we meet Carl and Scott. Carl is holding an improbably thick wad of cash, which he claims to have taken at knife-point from a local crook; he is looking to spend the money. Richie, whose giro is not due for another week, is happy to help. The three of them – Carl and Scott and Richie – head off down the high street together; over his shoulder, Richie tells me he'll call back at the hostel that evening to pick up his application form.

There is no sign of Richie that evening, nor the following morning. His job application sits on the desk in the staff office for several weeks until Philip throws it away. One month on, Ann gets a call from the housing association asking for news – Richie's room has been empty for over a fortnight. His whereabouts remain a mystery until Suzie, newly resident at the hostel and pining for her boyfriend Brian, returns from a prison visit with word that Richie is back 'inside'. This news is soon confirmed.

tom

thanks for righting. It's good to here from ya ... a lot has happed from the last time I saw you. I would very much like a visit from you.

I could be in court any time from the 27th ... I'll tell you allabout it when I see you. I'm a bit bigger becouse I've bin doing waghts and football every day. I'v had a cubble of fights. also I'v lost 7 days. but there was know way I was going to let any one mess with me when I'm in here. know what I mean. to be some one in prison you have to prove ya self and now I've gone that I'v got things running sweet. If I do go down I will be going to —— thatis a harder prison but ill be alright. any way tom have to go so take care.

Looking forward to seeing you.

Richie.

p.s. If you have a old tape recoder you don't use could I please borow it becouse I ant got any music my walkman don't work any more. if you havent thanks any way.

Hard on the heels of the news about Richie, another setback: Ryan returns to the hostel, evicted from his bedsit following a dispute about the fuel bill. He is hazy on the details and rather more casual about being back on Lime Street than the staff would like. He is no sooner booked in than he is off out to spend the evening with Roy. In the staff office, Kevin opens up the filing cabinet.

'The advice that we're giving them when they're here,' he says, thumbing through the files, looking for Ryan's old paperwork, 'they're not applying it once they get out there. That's the reason they come back. They come back, basically, to hear the same thing again; but they're not doing anything about it ... Once they leave us they go right back to Marlborough Hill and the surrounding areas and get back to that negative atmosphere again. Being that we don't have reins on them, we don't walk the streets with them, once they leave this house they're with that same negative crowd and all that we've done and said has been diluted by their friends ... If we had a situation where they were away from that environment then I think we would see more as far as the turnaround in their lives ... Like with Cherie, her friends play a big part – when she leaves here she's back with the negative atmosphere and friendships and so forth and that's what causes the cycle.'

*   *   *

The staff have seen this sort of thing too many times to be all that surprised or let down, but the problem remains. Away from the hostel, out there in 'bedsit land', things come undone: Cherie gets in with a 'druggie' crowd; Richie reoffends; Ryan lets things slip and is homeless again. The 'cycle of instability and home-lessness' (see page 23) that these young people are caught up in seems to have as much to do with the company they keep as anything else. The usual suspects are easily singled out – Dean and Tariq, Jones, Scott, Carl; but Kevin's is also a wider complaint. His final comments about 'Marlborough Hill and the surrounding areas' hint at a wider, careless pattern of low expec-tation and anti-social and irresponsible behaviour that seems somehow quorate in the bedsits, shared and shored up by pretty much everyone, by 'that same negative crowd ... their friends'.

Something Sticky

This takes us close to the heart of the underclass thesis, the idea that once in place, and howsoever arrived at, patterns of under-standing and practice common to some fraction of the poor adhere and hold fast, and a type of poverty establishes itself – a pattern of and for behaviour, a way of life perhaps. Young people who are more or less habituated to a life that revolves around benefits, hostels, bedsits and homelessness (or are at least headed in that direction) might seem a case in point, but it is the intro-duction of the glib phrase 'a way of life' that makes all the difference here, suggesting something other, and more, than that some of those at the margins might (have to) get used to living there.

It is culture that is being worked into the argument here; and culture is something shared and collectively affirmed, not just an aggregate concurrence of individual coping strategies and whatever else. As such, it has a coherence and dynamic all its own; it has momentum. Sufficient momentum, perhaps, to kick free of circumstance once and for all. That, at least, is the recurrent allegation; that some sort of scission and then closure has occurred, or is occurring, that members of an underclass – the homeless and 'disaffected' young, the long-term unemployed and welfare dependent, drug users, persistent offenders, inhabit-ants of 'sink estates' – have turned away from society and in on themselves, taking up ways of living that are of a piece and persistent. This was Murray's populist conclusion, having visited Britain in the late 1980s. He declared himself to be in no doubt that the country was host to 'a growing population of working-aged, healthy people who live in a different world from other Britons ... and whose values are now contaminating the life of entire neighbourhoods' (1990: 4); and he judged his suspicions confirmed on a subsequent visit (see Murray, 1994; also Buckingham, 1996).

This is strong language, and it is a language that shades off all too easily into moral judgement and blame. And yet there are those passing through the hostel – Joe, for one – whose lifestyles and life situations run close together; so close, sometimes, it is not always easy to tell the two apart.

Consensus

Setting aside any value judgement for the moment, there are good enough reasons for supposing that a collection of teenagers moving around the same grid of streets in the same town and struggling to get to grips with the same difficulties might, in the process, reach some sort of common understanding particular to their lived situation, a shared sense of how things stand and where that leaves them; there are good reasons too for supposing that this consensus might bed in somehow. Imagine a pristine scenario, with the bedsits standing empty awaiting a first cohort of young people just 'kicked out' of home. How long until two of those new tenants run into one another, relieved to meet someone else who is finding things just as tough as they are, someone making the same piecemeal concessions and adjustments here and there? How long until these two set about measuring up to, and making sense of, their situation together: arriving at solutions to everyday problems in collaboration, exploring the alternatives available to them with increasing confidence, sticking their necks out together perhaps a little further than they would were they on their own (Hannerz, 1992: 71)? Soon enough, surely. One could expect the very first stirrings of such a consensus to date from the first few days of occupancy.

As it is, there have been young people drifting through the same rented properties in Southerton for years; plenty of time for any such consensus to consolidate and wax reciprocal. When Kim insists that she

... like[s] working for the government at the moment, so I'm all right. Getting paid by the government for doing nothing, I'm satisfied with that for the moment, till I get myself sorted out ...

she does so knowing that others on Marlborough Hill already share her cynicism and are keeping their expectations on as tight a leash as she is. The same goes for Bagsy's indifferent commentary on his upcoming court appearance:

Bagsy: Life's a game, innit? You get in a couple of holes, you jump out again: it's a laugh, innit?

Statements like these draw on a shared understanding, distilled from common experience, without which they would fall flat. And that is not all they do: they also reinforce and extend that understanding such that some home truths about life in the bedsits, those that are rehearsed and remarked on in company almost daily and without significant contradiction, gain a momentum of sorts; an inertia, at least. Many more of the half-dozen young people sitting up against the radiator in Tracy's room on a wet December afternoon will subscribe to the view that 'jobs round here are not worth looking for' than have actually confirmed this for themselves in the last couple of weeks; even Leo nods his head, and he is not much more than a month out of school and barely knows his way to the Careers Service. Something here has edged ahead of itself, has secured a credibility that no longer turns on firsthand experience.[3]

And, of course, this is just the sort of thing that Kevin worries about. Young people who ought to be getting on in life are going nowhere instead, are holding each other back even. And that seems a shame. That shared reluctance to get along to the JobCentre is part of the problem – nothing will come of nothing.

3. Southerton is not an unemployment black-spot. If Cherie can land herself a job as a waitress then so can Tracy. Singly, any of those in Tracy's bedroom might do the same; might find a job, a job worth looking for even. But the odds of all six of them walking over to the JobCentre that afternoon and finding work are nil. At best, the JobCentre will have details of a couple of vacancies to which 16- and 17-year-olds with few qualifications and no experience or means of transport might apply – at best; and there are a great many more than that at the hostel and in the bedsits at any one time. In this sense the collective verdict that a trip to the JobCentre is a waste of time is entirely accurate: the jobs are not there.

And if it is not this, then it is Shane and Al egging each other on and ripping up their court summonses in the street or Adrian spending giro day with Jones and Vicky, two weeks' money gone up in smoke.

But what to do? There is little chance of young people like Leo or Ryan keeping to themselves once they leave the hostel, not if they are headed for a room on Stanley Street or Marlborough Hill. Life in the bedsits is lived at close quarters and within certain (narrow) limits. There are only so many things to do with not much money, only so many places to go. And the same people are there day after day: in line at the DSS, sat on the benches in the shopping centre, on their way across town to hang out at the hostel for a few hours. Besides which, friends are important, as much a lifeline as a liability, someone to talk to and borrow money from or stay overnight with. Getting by from one day to the next on Marlborough Hill means doing so together, and that means getting mixed up in one another's messy finances, housing difficulties and court appearances, and sharing in an indexical understanding of what all of this adds up to. And it does add up to something, for better or worse. Life on Marlborough Hill is not a shambles. Messy it may be, but it also works for those who live there, at least some of the time – as it has to do; and it hangs together somehow, at least some of the time – again, as it has to do. And for all that this may be a part of the problem, there is also something impressive here – infuriatingly so, as far Kevin is concerned, but impressive nonetheless; not so much 'negative' as resilient and embattled.

This is certainly true of the grit and savvy that have seen Joe through two years on the social margins, but it is true of a good deal else besides, and goes beyond a baseline survivalism of the sort that is a recurrent finding in studies of homelessness (see Carlen, 1996; Glasser and Bridgman, 1999: 58–89). There is a stubborn, insubordinate streak to life in the bedsits, one that sets itself *against* circumstances as much as it accommodates to them. Every day spent with Al and Shane is punctuated by petty acts of subversion and defiance in the face of authority. Al saunters into the Careers Service, sits down and lights up underneath the 'No Smoking' sign; Shane mutters insults at the security guards in the shopping centre, looking to provoke a confrontation; the two of them break into Al's landlord's flat and vandalise the place. At the end of the afternoon they are at the police station again, caught shoplifting. These two are *always* making trouble, for themselves and others. Not that it does them any good, but they do it anyway; this is the way they go at life; they dissent and kick against the pricks.

Full Circle?

In the early 1990s, in the same year as the Lime Street hostel first opened its doors, an umbrella group of housing and children's charities, the Young Homeless Group, published a leaflet stating clearly: 'Youth homelessness is a housing problem, not a reflection of the behaviour of young people today.' No one working at the Lime Street hostel would disagree. Young people come to Lime Street because they have nowhere else to go. It is a public shame that they should find themselves in such difficulties; things ought not to be that way. Whatever they might say amongst themselves in the privacy of the office, each and every member of the staff team would rebut any general suggestion that the young homeless are to blame for the mess they are in.

And yet the simple answer to Brian's rhetorical question, '[I]f I'm homeless and unemployed I want to get my life together, don't I?' (see page 43), is that not everyone leaving the hostel for a room on Victoria Road or Marlborough Hill does, or seems to want to. Some of them seem busy enough just passing time, 'working for the government' and hanging out together in the shopping centre – either this or they are caught up in some or other trouble of their own making and soon to be homeless again. The reasons why any of this happens are complicated, because homelessness is complicated. No one leaving Lime Street for the bedsits has things easy; money is tight, the rooms are shabby and it takes no time at all to get into difficulties. Many new tenants flounder. They lack experience and make mistakes; they get sidetracked and are glad of the distraction; they let themselves down sometimes. But they also bear up and make shift (on the back foot mostly, but not always so), and they do so together, in the company of friends who can be relied upon to see things the same way (at least some of the time) and in such a way that life in the bedsits, desultory as it is, holds together. Which is to say that there is – of course there is – a pattern of practice and interpretation squared (up) to and already a part of what it is like to live on Victoria Road or Marlborough Hill; something shared. It does not follow that anything here has come full circle – being poor is not so simple – but there it is all the same.

6
Coming of Age

At the close of Anthony Burgess' novel, *A Clockwork Orange*, Alex, the narrator and protagonist, finds himself growing up. Looking back on his days as a disaffected and vicious hooligan (and on the brutal 'cure' to which the authorities have subjected him), he concludes: 'And all it was was that I was young' (Burgess, 1972: 148).

The young are troubling to society, and not only as potentially spectacular delinquents. To be young at all is to be wilful, unthinking and irresponsible at times; this is one of the stereotypes we live by, and it is an enduring stereotype. Respectable fears about unruly younger generations are as old as, and mesh with, anxieties about the 'underserving' poor (see Pearson, 1983).[1] The enduring power of the young to disconcert owes something to the ambiguity of youth as an intermediary and transitional phase. Young people are betwixt and between. No longer children and not yet adults, they do not quite fit or fully belong; and this makes youth a rolling moment of social tension and unease.[2] But no one stays forever young. Young people grow older; they leave their youth and younger days behind them and move to maturity, majority and social integration. That is what is supposed to happen, at least; but this move does not always come easy.

British sociologists have had a lot to say on the subject of youth transitions over the last twenty years or so, not much of

1. Writing in the early seventeenth century, Shakespeare has an old shepherd complain: 'I would there were no age between ten and three-and-twenty, or that youth would sleep out the rest; for there is nothing in the between but getting wenches with child, wronging the anciently, stealing, fighting' (*The Winter's Tale* 3:3). The language is dated, but not the sentiment; consider just some of the media and moral panics of the last ten years or so: teenage pregnancy, underage drinking and drug use, young runaways, juvenile street crime (especially attacks on the elderly).
2. Anthropologists have long been sensitive to the significance of liminal positions and persons and their potential to disconcert (see Van Gennep, 1960; Leach, 1968; Turner, 1969; Douglas, 1984).

it good news. The general consensus seems to be that the passage to adulthood has become a much more complex, risky and potentially arduous undertaking for almost all young people (see Jones and Wallace, 1992; Morrow and Richards, 1996; Furlong and Cartmel, 1997).[3] If so, the young homeless can be assumed to be working a harder passage than most.

How much, then, of what seems troubling in the previous chapters, is best understood as a function of youth? Is it just that those passing through the Lime Street hostel are young? Does it follow that, as they grow up, they will leave behind them the lives they are leading now?

Because They're Young

When Ann sits Danny down in the staff office at the hostel and tells him that he is being catapulted into adulthood and that, aged 16, he is going to have to behave like a 20-year-old (see page 38), she is framing his predicament in a particular way and identifying a particular remedy: Danny is going to have to grow up, and fast. His problem is not so much that he is homeless but that he is 16 years old and homeless: he is young. And this explains a lot. After all, it is a contemporary common-sense that life is not easy for young people. Good jobs are hard to come by, training schemes are not all they are cracked up to be and leaving home is not an easy undertaking. Everyone knows this. Just as everyone knows that young people running the risks that come with starting out on their own in the world are sometimes the last to see the seriousness of their situation. If Danny or any other of the residents at the hostel appear headstrong, unthinking, contrary, irresponsible, or whatever else, then that is only to be expected:

> *Philip*: ... because they're young, and it's the first time they've probably been away from their family. Someone who's 16, 17, it's their first time, like, with no responsibility in the world, no parents to nag at them. They want to do what they want, and believe me they're going to come and go – do what they want. We're going to have to try hard enough just to get them in at eleven [i.e. in time for

3. Nor is this a peculiarly British finding (see Bynner *et al.*, 1997; Wyn and White, 1997).

bed]. So try saying to them to stay in and work on their literacy skills or whatever ... I mean, how many of them want to do it anyway? They have to want to do it for themselves.

Youth is important then, twice over; the fix Danny is in and his behaviour under the circumstances have something to do with being young. No one can blame him for that perhaps, but, all the same, he needs to get his act together; he is going to have to grow up. And it makes sense – means something – for Ann to tell him to do so.[4]

And if growing up is what it is all about, then who is going to argue with that? Growing up is something we all do, '[p]eople have *got* to grow up' (Hutson and Jenkins, 1989: 109; original emphasis); certainly, no 17-year-old wants to be treated like a child.

*   *   *

Michael is in the staff office boasting to Graham and Cherie about his joy-riding exploits. Ann is studiously ignoring all three of them, but Michael keeps it up, looking to get a reaction out of her – something about respect for other people's property or what if someone had been hurt. He likes to argue with Ann, but she is not playing ball. His boasts get louder and more outrageous and then Ann suddenly reaches out and grabs hold of him, sitting him on her lap like a baby.

'Oh dear!' she says, bouncing him on her knee. 'Aren't I listening? Do you want some attention Michael?'

Michael struggles desperately to get free.

'No! Get off. You're crazy you are.'

This is not what he wanted; everyone is laughing. Ann lets him go and he disappears upstairs.

A couple of days later Michael and Ann are at it again. Having spent all afternoon at the police station, Michael returns to the hostel in a bad mood, swearing and carrying on in a stagy way; the other residents are keeping out of his way. He stalks into the front room and kicks the coffee table. The table tips over; coffee cups fly and an ashtray smashes on the floor. This was rather more than he intended. Ann comes in from the office. She is in no mood for this. Aware that he has

---

4. Were their positions reversed, it would make little or no sense for Danny to tell Ann, who is 28 years old, to act as if she were 32.

overplayed his hand, Michael listens in silence as Ann reads him the riot act.

'I want all the bits of glass picked up, every one of them Michael, and then you are to leave the hostel. I won't tolerate that kind of behaviour here. You are not a baby to throw tantrums in this house; you're an adult, and you need to start behaving like one.'

Later that evening, with Michael back inside and upstairs in his bedroom, Ann is hoping she was not too hard on him; he is only 17, after all.

'Really, he needs to be allowed the privilege of having his childhood for another year and not having to go into the adult world so quickly. I feel for Michael.'

*   *   *

Michael does not have the luxury of acting his age; like Danny, he needs to grow up (until which time he can expect to be treated as a child). The sooner he does so, the sooner things will begin to sort themselves out; the longer he leaves it the harder things are going to get. But if Ann's sympathies are with Michael, there is less forbearance among the staff team for some of the hostel's older residents; those like Marky, who is back on Lime Street and now 20 years old, no longer a teenager.

> *Poppy*: Marky just drives me mad ... he's not a kid any more. He needs to start taking responsibility for his own life.
> *Philip*: He needs a good kick up the arse.

Of course there is a sense in which the very last thing that is happening to either Danny or Michael (or Marky, for that matter) is that they are being catapulted into adulthood. Growing up is hard enough as it is without being homeless, and if anything these two have their work cut out for them.[5] But this

5. Arguing along similar lines in the 1980s, Paul Willis suggested that high and rising youth unemployment might stall the transition to adulthood for a generation of school-leavers, leaving them more or less sidelined, dependent 'on state welfare, on ironically entitled "employment schemes" and on a sometimes unwilling family' (1984b: 476). The possibility of postponement, of social majority deferred, has echoed through the sociological and policy literature since then; but the idea that the young unemployed might be stuck forever shy of adulthood, like so many flies in amber, has been much qualified. An initially narrow focus on work and the wage as the passkeys to adulthood has flared out to allow a wider understanding of adulthood as a 'complex and multi-faceted social identity'

is Ann's point really. Michael is on his own and up against it, his parents are not on hand to help take the strain (see Hutson and Jenkins, 1989), and the question is: what is he going to do about it? Is he going to let things drift and go to pieces or is he going to start taking things seriously and take some responsibility? Ann knows what she wants to see: a sense of urgency and maturity, less of this childish behaviour. And putting it this way gets the message home sometimes. But not always. In truth, social majority is a reciprocal affair; Ann knows this and so does Michael. The local housing and jobs markets are skewed against young people in their teens, and the rules of benefit entitlement for 16- and 17-year-olds remain the same – 'complicated and harsh' (National Homeless Alliance, 1999: 302) – whether or not they act older than they are.

> *Barry*: The old winos are better off than we are ... they get loads of money man, they get fucking loads of money. This country don't give a shit about you if you're young.

And as for taking responsibility, not everyone on Lime Street feels that the responsibility is theirs to take, not all of it anyway. Go talk to Shelley's stepmum, or Michael's ex-landlord, or the government maybe.

Another side to this is that many of the young people who come to stay at the hostel consider themselves to be plenty old enough already, never mind how they choose to spend their time; not the adults that Ann would like them to be perhaps, but old enough not to have to take any lectures. As Shelley sees it, what she chooses to do with her life is her own business. She does

---

(Jenkins, 1990: 143), and various studies have shown that young people can and do grow up out of work and at the margins (see Coffield *et al.*, 1986; Wallace, 1987; Hutson and Jenkins, 1989), albeit with difficulty, passing a variety of personal, domestic, legal and other thresholds on the way to social majority. Leaving home is one such threshold *en route* to adulthood, and can be considered an important element of almost all young people's move into adulthood (see Morrow and Richards, 1996: 56), as important, in its way, as starting work. More than just a *consequence* of growing up, leaving home can be a *means* of doing so (Jones, 1995: 89), one of the ways in which young people can most visibly demonstrate and assert their independence – physically removing themselves from parental support and control. This is a step that many young people coming to Lime Street have already taken, as many of them claiming to have walked out of home as complaining they have been kicked out.

not want to hear about how she should be going back to college or upstairs tidying her bedroom. That was why she left home in the first place. What she wants for now is something else. She is 17 – not 12, not 20; and there is something about being 17 that seems worth holding on to. Difficult as the last few weeks have been for her, they have also been something of an adventure. Leaving home, moving from one sofa to the next, getting into various scrapes, sharing rooms at the hostel, signing on for the first time, dividing her afternoons between Marlborough Hill and the shopping centre, making new friends in low places: all of this has had its own passing appeal and heady excitement. Now, six weeks into her stay at the hostel, she has plans to leave Lime Street for a bedsit just off Victoria Road – not the nicest room, but just around the corner from where Siobhan and Al are staying. And she is excited just to be moving again; looking forward to having her own key, staying out late and sleeping in – all of this is new. Less so for Barry, who is the same age as Shelley, but has been in and around the bedsits (and on the streets) for almost six months now. He is not so green, and has done a good deal of growing up, by his own reckoning; not least during the weeks he spent living rough in London.[6] All the same, he is nothing if not 17 – smart-mouthed and impulsive, by turns surly and irrepressible, forever in some new tangle with the police or the DSS; he sprints up and down stairs.

Something of this same youthful seam runs right the way through life on Lime Street and Marlborough Hill. At the hostel, the residents are either noisily bored or rowdy and overexcited; in the bedsits, they are energetically unhappy – fretful; on the streets, they loiter and mooch and get in the way and stir things up. In amidst the uncertainty and anxiety, never far away, there is always this same energy and immediacy and, above all, a shared, coltish intensity whose taproot is a restless dissatisfaction with home and family and authority. For all that being young means being hard done by and pushed to the margins (and this has certainly been Barry's experience), it is also one of the few things that they have going for them – being young; that and

6. And he takes some pride in this, in his proven ability to look after himself, to cope – a concept which Liddiard points to as playing 'a critical role in the attainment of adulthood' (1990: 74).

one another. Better homeless, broke and young – 16 or 17 – than homeless, broke and old, one of the 'winos'.

For anyone coming to stay on Lime Street there is a sense in which homeless is already a grown-up thing to be.[7] But it does not follow that Shelley or Barry or any other of those at the hostel or on Marlborough Hill are in a rush to be *too* grown up about it. Whatever the hostel staff have to say, there is something about being 17 that seems worth holding on to. Jones certainly thinks so.

*   *   *

It is late afternoon on Lime Street, nearly time for the hostel to open. Jones is standing outside, talking with Ian and Darren. He has a black eye, which he claims he got off Vicky's dealer, although the truth is that it was Vicky who hit him. He and Vicky have been falling out and fighting a lot recently. Last week saw a short suspension of hostilities when Vicky announced that she was pregnant, but she has since revealed that this was a false alarm, 'a phantom pregnancy thing'. Jones wants out, and is asking if there are vacancies at the hostel.

Poppy pulls up in her car, gets out, and sets about unlocking the front door. Darren and Ian push past her to get the kettle on and reserve their place on the sofa. Jones cadges a cigarette from Poppy and starts up a conversation on the doorstep.

'I've had enough', he says. 'Vicky's doing my fucking head in. Maybe I'll come back and stay here. What do you think, Poppy?'

The phone is already ringing in the staff office, and Poppy has heard this from Jones before. 'I think you should try growing up a bit Jones,' she tells him, 'and facing up to some of your responsibilities instead of running away from things every time it gets hard'.

'I don't want to grow up though', Jones shouts after her as she closes the door. 'I want to be 17 again. I'll be 17 forever, me. You're as old as you feel, Poppy.'

*   *   *

7. Anyone who has ever had to sleep rough knows that homelessness is not child's play; it is a serious business, requiring fortitude and resourcefulness (see Richie's comments on pages 78–9). Likewise unemployed; to be out of a job is to be old enough to be working, and as such it is an adult status of sorts (if not a desirable one, ordinarily) entailing certain adult competencies and, for those claiming benefit, the management of a small but independent income (see Hutson and Jenkins, 1989: 108).

As it happens, Jones had it particularly hard when he was 17, not least *because* he was 17. All the same, things seemed different then, easier somehow; and he would like to feel that way, be that age, again.

Slowing Down

One day – more than likely – and whether or not he acts that way at 16, Danny will turn 20; he and Michael both. No one is 16, or 17, for ever. But it does not follow that life will be all that much easier for either of these two, or for Shelley or Barry, with their teens behind them. Three or four years is a long time, of course; all sorts of things could happen, and few, if any, of the residents are looking that far ahead. Ask Shelley what she thinks she will be doing in six months' or a year's time and she will trip out an easy answer – 'I know what I'm going to do: get a job and that. There's no way I'll be homeless in a year' – but, other than when replying to (pointless) questions such as this, she has no real plans at all; not beyond next Thursday, when her giro is due. And the truth is that twelve months down the line she could be little or no further on, still piecing together an income on benefits in some or other ratty bedsit room, maybe even back at the hostel. Even so, something will have changed.

*   *   *

It is two days before Richie is due to leave the hostel, two weeks until his twentieth birthday. He and Ann are in the staff office, drinking coffee. Ann wants to know what she should do about Richie's new roommate, Roy. Roy is 16, and since arriving on Lime Street a week ago he has hardly spent any time around the place; he slips out most mornings before doing his chores and comes back to eat dinner only to disappear again for the rest of the evening. Ann has not been able to get him to sit down with her for more than five minutes. This morning, looking for Siobhan's missing CDs, she has discovered a pile of stolen sportswear under Roy's bed. She thinks it may be best simply to phone the police and let him face the consequences. Richie is not so sure.

'I was like that when I was his age', he explains. 'Shoplifting and that. He says he's going to stop when he's 17, but I've told him it don't work like that. At 17 they'll throw the book at you. I understand why he's doing it though. I mean, he's had it hard. He's like that cos he has to be. You should talk to him like you did to me when I first come here. It takes time though; it won't work straight away. When you're 16 all you're thinking about is money, sex, drugs and that. You just want money – loads of it. You know, for going out and clothes and that.'

Ann glances at me; she knows I am finding the conversation interesting. She asks Richie to explain some more, but the doorbell rings and when she gets up to answer it Richie follows her out into the hallway.

*   *   *

Roy and Richie have a lot in common, sharing a room at the hostel as they do; but Richie sees a real difference too. Roy's brassy disaffection and verve, the loose, cocky confidence he has in himself, his casual disregard for the welfare and criminal justice professionals forever at his heels – all this has to do with his being 16. Young is the way he is. Richie, on the other hand, is 19 pushing 20 and one more arrest away from a return to prison. His room for manoeuvre is not what it was when he first left home.

Some evenings it can be hard to get through five minutes' conversation in the office without the doorbell ringing – residents, ex-residents and friends, chiefly, slipping in and out. When Ann breaks off from her talk with Richie to get the door she can be pretty sure it will be Craig or Graham, back from the corner shop, either that or Louise calling by to drink coffee and watch television; it could be the police, or the referral from the ABC project who was supposed to have called two hours ago, but that is about it really. Only, every so often, the staff get a surprise and open the door to someone they used to know and had forgotten all about: an ex, ex-resident. Like Janet, who calls in, wheeling a baby and pushchair, on a wet Saturday afternoon almost a year on from when she was last seen or heard of on Lime Street. She is living across town now and is getting married next month. 'This place hasn't changed', she says, flopping down on the chair with the broken armrest. Only it has. The front room is full of strangers – Adrian, Stephen, Mandy, William, Tara; other than Ann there is no one there she knows. It is the same when Simon returns from London, expecting to pick up where he left off five months ago. No one is at the old addresses any more, and the only familiar face at the hostel is Tracy, who is visiting for the evening and busy making toast in the kitchen. She has snippets of news, but nothing much: Vicky and Jones are still together, Marky is due in court on Wednesday, Scott was back at the hostel a week ago; that is about all she knows for sure.

What has happened to the others, where have they gone? The answer is that most of them have not gone anywhere, not far anyway. A few have moved away (or been taken out of circulation), but only a few; most are still living locally. Of these, some have made amends and moved back home, but the rest – a good number – are still in rented accommodation in and around the town centre; the difference being that, one way or another, they have slowed down a little.

> *Tracy*: I haven't seen Melanie for ages. She's still around, I know that. But she's slowed down a lot since last summer. I never see her. Not since she stayed [at Number 10 Victoria Road] that time. She's living near where Alan is now. I think she's got a job in ——— or somewhere.

Slowing down means just that – a change of pace. Melanie has been keeping out of trouble and away from Victoria Road, away from the hostel too; it is two months since she last paid a visit to Lime Street. Ann and Kevin think maybe they have seen the last of her, although you can never tell for sure. When I run into her at the ABC project a week later, with boyfriend Nigel in tow, she tells me she has plans to go back to college in the autumn. Her dad has promised to help out financially if she gets back into education – she is talking to her dad again, after almost a year of silence. She laughs when I tell her that Simon is back at the hostel and asking after her. 'I'm well out of all that', she says.

This is a different Melanie from the one who first came to stay on Lime Street. Back then, as Ann remembers, she was 'nothing but trouble ...' – stroppy and difficult in key-work sessions, always falling out and fighting with Tracy (or out shoplifting together, the two of them), evicted from two properties in as many days in her first week away from the hostel – '... a real tearaway'.[8] But not any more. Now she is leaving all that behind. Not that she

---

8. All this long before Cherie and Tara arrived on the scene. 'Cherie and Tara are pretty much Melanie and Tracy all over again', says Ann.

is out of the woods just yet, but she is settled somewhere and has a few things going for her – a job, some plans for the future. And sometimes that is all it takes, just a few things coming together at the right time. Jamie was the same, as bad as Melanie and worse – incorrigible – and then he moved in with his sister and started working weekends at a petrol station, and that was that.

It is always a boost for the hostel staff to hear that an ex-resident like Melanie is doing all right for herself; 'getting a grip', as Ann likes to say. For Kevin it all comes down to finding work.

> *Kevin*: They need to ... go to the JobCentre and find a job, that is the only thing that is going to get them off the ground.

And Melanie would agree, at least in part. Having a job has made a big difference, and she was lucky to get a job at all (it was Nigel's mum who got her in where she is now, working as a part-time care assistant in a nursing home). But she feels it has taken time too, and this as much as anything else. There was no stopping her, she says, when she first left home. But after a year or more in the thick of things she was about ready to slow down, job or no job.

> *Melanie*: I'd had enough anyway, know what I mean? It was doing my head in, all that.

Ten months on from leaving home, and back on Lime Street for a second time, Pete is starting to see things the same way.

> *Pete*: Time to slow down really, know what I mean? I'm getting too old for all this. I did [slow down] in a way before I come back here, not really though. But now I have, quite a lot really – had to really. I don't do nothing no more, not now.

Things are hardly looking up for Pete; if anything, he is in a tighter spot than when he first stayed at the hostel.

> *Pete*: The police know me now; they know me. At the station it's like: 'You again is it? Right, in you go.'

The local landlords know him too and he is barred from numerous properties on and around Marlborough Hill. 'It's all right for Darren and them,' he says, nodding at the noise coming from the staff office where Darren and Ian, both 16, are arguing with Poppy, 'but not for me, not any more, I need to get my life sorted.' After the best part of a year spent homeless on and off and in conspicuous difficulties, he is tired of the aggravation.

Whether Pete will manage to keep out of trouble remains to be seen, but Ann is more hopeful than she was six months ago. Of course, it would have been better if he had been talking this way when he first arrived on Lime Street, but this is something the staff team have had to get used to. Working with the young homeless is more of a waiting game than Ann lets on to either Danny or Michael. Tara is into her third stay on Lime Street – her ban lifted following an appeal from the social services – before the staff begin to see a change in her.

> *Ann*: So I'm going to have a key-working session with Tara tonight ... I know she's talked to you too about feeling depressed at the moment. I think in a way that's positive for Tara, cos she's not, you know, blagging and the normal stuff. She's getting a grip on reality now. It's time for her to grow up, I think.

Tony is into his fifth stay.

> *Tony*: Now, hopefully, I can find a nice place to live, settle down, carry on working hard on my work placement until I manage to get a job – fingers crossed. Some things are working out all right, but other things aren't. People like Al are just living the dosser's life, on the dole. I was like that for a year and a half and now I'm coming to my senses. I need to do something. Sitting round town's just a waste of time.

This is a start then, but it has been a long time coming, and is hardly the acceleration of responsibility, the 'turnaround in their lives', that Kevin and Ann would work if they could. Pete has not so much settled down as run out of steam and options; Tara is demoralised; some things are working out all right for Tony, others aren't. Each of them is now older than when they first came to Lime Street.

At 18, Pete might seem a little too young to be getting 'too old' for anything, but he is older than he was – older, this time around, than most of the other residents at the hostel; and if things are catching up with him then this is one of the ways in which that is happening. Darren and Ian are not much more than a year or so younger than he is, but the gap is there. And wider still for a young man like Raymond.

*   *   *

A call from a London hostel, a referral: Raymond, just out of prison and looking to move away from the capital. He arrives on Lime Street, already apprised of the routines and regulations of hostel life, having stayed in plenty before, but a little disconcerted to find that, at 22, he is by far and away the oldest resident in a house full of teenagers, most of them five or six years his junior. When Paul arrives at the hostel a week later, he and Raymond quickly team up; Paul is 19 years old, which is something, and has stayed at other hostels too – he 'knows the score', says Raymond. Between the two of them they reorganise the bedrooms to secure a room of their own together. Around the hostel they keep aloof from the resident group, sometimes adopting a mock-parental concern for the younger residents; especially David, the youngest, who is keen to impress but never quite sure when he is being baited.

Raymond and Paul are on the sofa watching television. David is bobbing and weaving in front of the screen, trying to persuade one or other of them to walk into town with him; he is due at the police station in half an hour to receive a formal caution.

'A caution I'm getting, like I'm supposed to be fucking grateful.'

Raymond shakes his head gravely. 'You're easily led, that's your problem David. Your problem is that you're easily led.'

David is unsure what to make of this. 'Fuck you', he ventures.

'And you're swearing too much. Give it a rest.'

Again a pause, and then: 'Kiss my arse.'

Raymond says nothing. David busies himself trying to flick his lighter open and alight in a single movement, the way he has seen the others do.

'You're smoking too much David, you know that?' says Paul.

Now David knows the joke is on him. He moves to the door and flicks his lit cigarette across the room at the pair of them. 'Fuck off, motherfuckers. I'll do what I want.'

Raymond makes a sudden start, as if to stand up and give chase. David turns to sprint for the kitchen. Catching his foot on the carpet tread, he trips and sprawls in the corridor.

'Watch yourself there David', says Raymond from his chair, with equanimity.

'Fuck you.'

David picks himself up, adjusts the headphones to the personal stereo he carries with him at all times, and swaggers off.

After three weeks at the hostel, Raymond moves out to a rented room on Springfield Avenue. A couple of days later, Paul follows him, taking up the offer of space on the floor. For a month or so their room becomes a hub for visitors from the hostel and other bedsit rooms nearby; David is always hanging around there, coming back to the hostel last thing at night, high as a kite. Then, two months on from arriving in Southerton, Raymond leaves. He calls round to my room to say goodbye, and tells me he has plans to head to a hostel in the next town, somewhere he has stayed before, and from there to South London, where a friend of his was living, last he heard. This will leave Paul in the lurch, but he has made his mind up. He thinks maybe David will move in and they can sort something out between them. When I ask him why, he has no real reason to hand. We talk around it for a while.

'I've just had better times than this, you know', says Raymond. 'I mean, I'm fine here; I'm just bubbling along. But I've had better times. They're all so young in the bedsits, and with the drugs and stuff, they're just learning stuff that I've already learned.'

* * *

Raymond is finding things hard just when he ought to be finding things easy. After all, he has been here before, if not in Southerton. He is no stranger to hostel life, and yet he is hardly one of the crowd on Lime Street. His age and experience, not least the kudos that comes with having been 'inside', afford him some standing among the younger residents; but the price paid for this is distance. The humour in his exchanges with David is premised on this – on Raymond's dry seniority and David's junior impertinence. Away from the hostel it takes him no time at all to carve out a familiar space for himself on Springfield Avenue, but back in the bedsits he has been drifting through since he left local authority care years ago, he is soon enough finding things a little *too* familiar; so much so that he feels himself to be getting out of touch.

This is the problem, and not just for Raymond but for Marky and Pete and Tony and any others who have been around the bedsits and in difficulties long enough – a little too long – and are not kids any more. There are, of course, tenants of all ages on Marlborough Hill, Catherine Street and Springfield Avenue, but the bedsits really belong to, and are most conspicuously occupied by, the youngest of these; those newly arrived, still learning stuff and making trouble. Although Raymond has no difficulty making himself at home on Springfield Avenue, it is David who fits right in there. At 16 and 17 it makes a sort of sense for David and Darren and Ian, and any other of the new arrivals on Lime Street, to be the way they are and act like they do – to mess around with drugs and petty crime, pitching from one bedsit room to another and in and out of hostels. Being young lends itself to being in this sort of trouble, even makes this sort of trouble fun sometimes. This is not *why* anyone on Lime Street is homeless – if it were, Raymond's problems would be over; but it is very much *how*.

7
Conclusion

Is youth homelessness really no more than a housing problem, as the Young Homeless Group has it (see page 115), nothing to do with the behaviour of the young homeless themselves? The answer is yes and no. In Southerton at any rate, there is a sense in which housing is the least of it. There are almost always rooms to rent on Marlborough Hill or Stanley Street, certainly so if you can wait a week or two, at the hostel or on someone's sofa, and are prepared to take what you can get. Only this is where the problems seem to start (up again) for so many of the young people leaving Lime Street, back in what Marky calls 'bedsit land' – and soon enough, some of them, homeless again and broke – not that homeless and broke is what Marky or any of the others want to be.

Seven weeks into his residency at the hostel Matt may be no closer to finding a place of his own than when he first arrived (see pages 43–4), but the truth is that he was never all that far away. And sure enough, with only a few days to spare, and with Ann's help and some money from his social worker, he manages to find a room on Catherine Street recently vacated by Paula. Pleased as they are with this outcome, neither Ann nor his social worker (who has supplied him with money for a deposit on two previous occasions) imagines he will stay put. Ann's best guess is that the problems that have dogged Matt since he left local authority care six months ago – the drugs, the car thefts, the company he keeps, his seeming inability to manage his finances – will as likely as not disrupt his accommodation again, and before too long. It does not help that the room he has moved to is not up to much and that his security of tenure is effectively nil, but if only he would keep out of trouble and get his act together, lose that attitude. A job would be a start, any job at all, but Matt is barely qualified and shows little interest or enthusiasm. None of his friends are working.

Bad Language: Culture and Poverty

Back in the staff office, having waved Matt goodbye, Ann is anxious that the hostel has given him little more than a respite, and that he will not so much settle down now as disappear off the map for a few more weeks or months, resurfacing on Lime Street sooner or later, looking for somewhere to stay again.

> *Ann*: He should be going over to the ABC project right now [to fill in the application forms for college that Ann has been helping him with] ... but I've a feeling that he's just going to disappear into the abyss again. But really that's, that's all we can do ...

'Into the abyss' is laying it on a bit thick perhaps; it calls to mind Jack London's grim account of London's East End a century ago, *The People of the Abyss* (1998; originally 1903). Not that we are any the less anxious today about the causes and consequences of poverty and the character of the urban poor (see Byrne, 1999); nor are the young homeless any the less exemplars of social exclusion in the twenty-first century than they were a hundred years ago. Ann's worry is not so much that Matt is about to descend into an underworld of poverty and squalor, rather that he is likely to slip back into some localised cycle of disadvantage, of which homelessness is the most visible, recurrent feature. Not an abyss then, more a pocket or eddy of misbehaviour and disaffection that could keep Matt in difficulties for some time to come and spoil his future.

Does this tally then with what Nick Davies has to say in *Dark Heart*, about 'what academics like to call subcultures ... little colonies, looking inwards at their own values and rituals, their own ways of surviving' (1998: 236)? The closest I have come to saying so is in Chapter 5, where I have described a consensus, a loose agreement as to what is expedient, opportune and admissible under the circumstances, elements of which, because fitted to life on Marlborough Hill, run counter to norms for conduct as these apply elsewhere and more widely.

So do we call this culture, or subculture perhaps; and what does it matter if we do? If by culture we mean no more than that process whereby people with everyday lives in common make a shared sense of how they live them, then the answer is yes, certainly this is culture, and why not? Culture thus defined is not that big a deal after all, it happens all the time:

> Whenever some group of people have a bit of common life with a modicum of isolation from other people, a common corner in society, common problems and perhaps a couple of common enemies, there culture grows. (Hughes, 1961: 28, quoted in Hannerz, 1992: 62)

Agreed. Culture is not an aberration, in itself wrong or reprehensible – negative.[1] It is an ordinary and circumstantial process, something we all do – make sense of things, together, and from where we are standing. Nevertheless, it has a certain reach and hold over those in its midst, providing as it does an indexical basis for the ongoing assessment and interpretation of events. It also plucks at those who are new on the scene. As I have already suggested, the most solitary and unsociable of tenants would struggle to spend a week on Victoria Road or Stanley Street without some exposure to the modes of behaviour that pass current there.[2] An afternoon spent with Jones and Vicky is an education. This is what maddens Kevin. Away from the hostel and in with that 'negative' crowd, young people like Ryan catch on quick and get into the way of things; and then, three months later, sure enough, they are back on Lime Street or up in front of the magistrates.

If this is a problem – and it certainly looks like a problem from where Kevin is standing – it is not *the* problem. Not unless the

---

1. It is a conspicuous weakness of the more lurid descriptions of an underclass, that the various traits of character and lifestyle bundled together under the heading 'culture' – dependency, disaffection, apathy, indiscipline, irresponsibility – are wholly antithetic. Such an unremittingly negative portrayal works against itself. What is there here that anyone might affirm and make their own? This is culture only in silhouette: an inversion of normative values and behaviour, a scare story.
2. Consider the hours that Jono keeps (see page 106). He may have his own reasons for sleeping late most mornings, good reasons as he sees them, but it is hardly lost on him that no one else he knows is up until midday. 'Nothing happens, not until the afternoon', he says. 'There's no point calling on anyone until the afternoon, not unless they've had their giro.' This is only to be expected. As Malinowski puts it, inverting Kant, '[t]he real rule guiding human behaviour is this: "what everyone else does ... this is right, moral and proper. Let me look over the fence and see what my neighbour does, and take this as a rule for my behaviour"' (1978: 326–7).

suggestion is that something here has curled all the way back on itself such that the question why – why any of this happens – can be answered without looking elsewhere. Culture thus defined is a much bigger deal and does not happen all the time, if indeed it ever really happens at all. It certainly does not happen on Marlborough Hill, which is no more a world closed in on itself than it is any more than ten minutes' walk from the JobCentre or the train station; not that the distance really matters. What matters is that to the extent that life on Marlborough Hill takes on any shape at all it does so in consequence of the subordinate position it occupies within a wider societal context. Life on Marlborough Hill is not just difficult, it is inferior, second rate; that is its defining characteristic. Stuck on the dole in bedsit or hostel accommodation is no one's idea of the good life at the end of the day. Attempts to skirt around this or brazen it out somehow are just that, and they hold good to a varying extent and falter altogether sometimes.

*   *   *

It is early evening. Alan has been arrested and Samantha and I head over to the police station to find out what is happening. Walking through the town centre together, someone shouts out after us. Scott sticks his head out of a fogged-up phone booth, clouds of smoke escaping around him as he beckons us over. He is full of the joys of giro day.

'Fucking great day', he says. 'Fuck court tomorrow, you know what I mean? I've got a beer in one hand, a spliff in the other, I'm going to give my new girlfriend a ring, have her come round. Who could ask for more?'

Scott wants us to come back with him to his bedsit. His enthusiasm is infectious, but Samantha is just not in the mood. We leave him to make his phone call, promising to maybe call by later.

Standing outside the police station, smoking cigarettes and waiting for news, we get talking. The past few weeks have been difficult for Samantha. She has fallen out with her family again and has been staying away from home, sleeping on a succession of friends' floors for most of this time. Yesterday the ABC project managed to find her a place to stay, but she is not happy there.

Poppy took her to the JobCentre this morning to have a look around, but there didn't seem to be anything she could apply for. All of the vacancies were for someone older, with more experience. For a while, Poppy had her thinking about maybe going back to school to resit her GCSEs, but she has gone off the idea now.

'I was crap at school anyway. I'm confused, I don't know what to do with my life.'

She went to see her doctor last week, she tells me, and he has referred her to a counsellor: her first session is a month away. She is broke and desperate for a change of clothes.

'I really feel like killing myself', she tells me. 'I don't show it though.'[3]

*   *   *

Many more of Southerton's young homeless have felt this way once in a while than care to admit it ordinarily. Jones is as much a part of the bedsit crowd as anyone, but this does not stop him wishing he and Vicky lived anywhere else (see page 72). If Samantha is going to stick it out on her own in the bedsits she will have to do as others have done: rein in her expectations and busy herself with getting by; either that or just stop worrying about tomorrow and let things slide, like Scott. Not that Scott hasn't had his bleak moments too; there is a measure of much the same desperation as Samantha is feeling, not too far below the surface of his hedonism. But not only desperation. His casual dismissal of all but the here and now – 'Fuck court tomorrow' – is not only an indiscipline but also a provocation, a deliberate affront to any who might want to take it that way: a refusal to take his situation seriously or lying down.

Most of the young people passing through the hostel, certainly those, like Scott, who have been struggling on their own and homeless for any length of time, share a suspicion that they have been let down somehow, by society or 'the system', and this gives their behaviour and bearing a jagged edge. As much as they struggle to make do under the circumstances, they struggle also

3. Three of the young people I first met at the Lime Street hostel did try to kill themselves during the year I spent in Southerton, each under different circumstances and for ostensibly very different reasons (Samantha was not one of these). This figure does not include a handful of drug-related incidents (overdoses, mostly) where individuals seriously endangered their own lives, but where I do not think there was an intention to attempt suicide.

against those circumstances; they dissent, in myriad ways, picking their targets wildly at times. There is a raw politics here,[4] and perhaps culture too, as something other than shared adaptation: culture as a means and mode of resistance.

Accommodation and dissent are woven closely together in the bedsits, so closely as to be indistinguishable at times. Reporting a girocheque stolen every once in a while works both ways: it brings in a little extra cash *and* it gets one over 'the system'. Quitting his room on Stanley Street Max appears to take the line of least resistance, but there is protest here too, a stubborn refusal to accommodate or settle. And then there is the 'attitude' that Poppy cannot abide, the surly, streetwise, contrary manner in which almost anything in the bedsits gets done: the tone Vicky takes at the Post Office, the studied inattention with which Stephen flicks his cigarette butts across the polished floor of the magistrates court. If some or all or any of this seems negative, uncalled for, then that is just the point. Nothing comes of nothing, but a refusal is not nothing. To say no, to dissent, is to say and do something at least; it is an affirmative, human act, and necessary as such.[5] These are the moments around which life on Marlborough Hill turns.

Culture and resistance make for a heady brew, but there are harder questions to ask of resistance than that of how many different practices it can be shown to reside in. Tara's careless economy (see page 106) may well be dissent of a sort, a spend-thrift refusal to measure out her life in small change, but it does not get her anywhere much at the end of the day. It is important

4. Certainly so in some of the more dramatic confrontations between Southerton's young homeless and the public authorities (DSS officials and the police), but also in the piecemeal insubordination that Al and Shane and many others routinely engage in; what James Scott calls small arms fire, 'the ordinary weapons of relatively powerless groups: foot dragging; dissimulation ... pilfering' (1985: xvi).

5. It is very hard to reason the need in this context; what is necessary and what is not; what is negative or needless. Stripped down to bare necessity, life on Marlborough Hill would amount to very little. What gives it its meaning and substance are those moments where it overflows the mark. In this context, surfeit takes on an urgency and importance, dissent a necessity. But then bare necessity – endurance, accommodation, survival – is its own protest. 'The strength to deny ... this strength we possess always, but not the courage; and yet life itself is denial, and therefore denial affir-mation' (Kafka, 1994: 46).

also to recognise the subjective ambivalence of those engaged in acts of resistance (Ortner, 1995: 175); what it is they think they're up to and why. Vicky goes shoplifting almost every other day, but the reasons she does so are many, and her feelings about this activity ambivalent. Sometimes she goes out 'on the rob' of necessity, because there is no food in the fridge; sometimes she does so just to get out of the house and maybe pamper herself a little. Sometimes Tara calls round and the two of them head into town together 'on a mission', coming home buzzing at having turned the tables on the high street stores. Most days she insists there is nothing wrong with stealing, 'not from the shops anyway'; shoplifting is something she is good at (she has never once been caught). But there are times when she is less sure of herself:

> *Vicky*: I don't like to do it, not really; it's nothing to be proud of ... It wasn't so bad when I was 16, I suppose.

And the same holds true for almost anything in that same repertoire of behaviours that Vicky and others draw on daily. Mostly it is a question of time and place. When Cherie gets a job at a pizza restaurant she rushes to the hostel to tell Ann the good news and phone her parents; when she is sacked she spends the afternoon getting high and watching television with Dean, insisting that she was going to leave anyway. In the shopping centre, playing cat and mouse with the security guards, Al is brimming with confidence; the next day, now facing a court appearance, he is regretting ever having gone there: 'Stupid, I should never have done it.' If no one spending the afternoon at Tracy's feels all that enthusiastic about looking for work that is not because they have set their faces against the work ethic once and for all, it is just that jobs are hard to find – no one has to spend all day looking to know that; and anyway it is raining outside, and with Lisa due back soon with cigarettes no one is about to up and leave for the JobCentre just yet. Kim's brash statement about life on the dole tails off into mitigation, finishing weakly with the proviso '... till I get myself sorted out'. And this is the sort of thing one hears daily at the hostel, on Victoria Road and outside the DSS: 'I'm giving it at least a few weeks'; '... tomorrow maybe'; '... when I've got a place of my own'.

Which is not to say that everything disappears into a general confusion. Life in the bedsits has a way about it, doubtless; but the shared understandings that underwrite this are strained, equivocal and sensitive to context (Howe, 1998: 532), as one would expect. This is hardly the place at which to begin an informed understanding of why it is that Kim or Marky lead the lives that they do, why it is they are homeless. Any assumption that it might be, that people with everyday lives and under-standings, with culture, in common might usefully constitute a unit of analysis such that a description of that culture would adequately describe their life circumstances, is not really on, and has not been on for some time (Keesing, 1981: 480).[6] Social scientists – sociologists and anthropologists alike – have long since moved away from any such understanding – culture as a closed circuit of values and behaviour, an isolate lump of sameness (Geertz, 2000: 254); and they have done so, in part, in the context of close argument about the lives of the urban poor (see Valentine, 1968; also Howe, 1990). This is what makes talk of little colonies and ways of life so very unconvincing, as a soci-ological proposition at least. The portrayal of an underclass, or any subcultural fraction thereof, as bricked up behind its own way of life is simply clumsy; it is uninformed.

Homeless Youth

So much then for (sub)culture. Which leaves youth. And this is, young is, what Tara and Al and Dean most obviously are. They are teenagers, young offenders, care-leavers and school-leavers; young, and unsettled. Young is the *way* they are too. Youth gives life on Lime Street and Marlborough Hill much of its particular character (such as it is), braiding trouble with fun (see Hebdige, 1988: 19) in such a way as is immediately recognisable and socially appreciable.

Nick Davies' exposé of Britain's dark heart takes its title from Joseph Conrad's *Heart of Darkness* – a novella of colonial adventure to the dark, definitively distant places of the earth. If

6. Keesing adds that this assumption 'may be doubly inappropriate to marginal subgroups in a complex class system' (1981: 480). He is commenting here on Spradley's classic study of homelessness and alcoholism, *You Owe Yourself a Drunk* (2000; originally 1970).

there is nothing of this alterity on Marlborough Hill, then a better one of Conrad's stories to set alongside the lives described here might be *Youth: A Narrative*. The two stories share the same central character: Marlow, a seaman. *Youth* is an account of a botched and sorry journey to deliver a cargo to its port of destination in the East in a battered old ship, the *Judea*. The journey is a failure. The ship springs leaks and is taken back to dock for repairs and then, finally under way, the 600-ton cargo of smouldering coal ignites, forcing the crew to abandon ship and make for shore in small boats. It is a story about coming of age. At one level, the ship stands for the family: the whole thing comes apart, and for the captain this feels like the end of the road. But for Marlow, a young second mate, the whole trip is an adventure.

> But you here – you all had something out of life: money, love – whatever one gets on shore – and, tell me, wasn't that the best time, that time when we were young at sea; young and had nothing, on the sea that gives nothing, except hard knocks – and sometimes a chance to feel your strength – that only – what you all regret? (Conrad, 1995: 43)

This is a romantic convention; youth as a time of high, unanchored excitement, a time for living dangerously. But we live by these and other conventions: they have a social validity, and, as such, an objective reality. People get into difficulties with their housing at all ages, young and old; but there is something *about* youth homelessness. There are good reasons why young people find themselves homeless in the numbers that they do; but over and above that, they do so at a time of life that is commensurate with unsettled circumstances. Youth, as a restless and intersticial age, is congruent with – thrums with – the uncertainty of life in and between temporary hostel and bedsit accommodation. Sixteen years old and unsettled is a thing to be – each bears the other out.

There is, of course, a trade-off taking place here, a settlement that romances, and thereby obscures, the hardships and inequalities of youth. Bourdieu argues along these lines, suggesting that the subordinate social position occupied by (all) young people results less from explicit oppression than it does from a more subtle transfer in which the 'ideological representation of the division between young and old grants certain things to the youngest, which means that in return they have to leave many things to their elders' (1993: 94). Thus, young people are granted a monopoly of sorts on qualities such as spontaneity and vitality, in order that other abilities and attributes are withheld from them – maturity, knowledge, power, seniority. These are the rules of the game: youth is a problem, a reckless and careless, effervescent age, and at the same time, and as such, an accommodation. This is how society compensates for the inferiority of youth; minority is traded for licence – a certain elbow-room and the power to discomfort, temporarily. And only temporarily.[7]

And then what? What happens next? What has happened to the 246,000 young people who were homeless in 1995? The answer is we do not know. We can be sure that only a few of these were homeless for all that long; probably no more than the smallest fraction were still homeless in 1996. But we can be just as sure that other young people have since taken their place. We can be sure that thousands of young people in their mid to late teens are homeless today.

Homelessness is – usually, thankfully – a temporary problem. It is temporary, first and foremost, because homeless is something most young people would rather not be, and where they see their way clear to doing so they put it behind them. Some take longer to do so than others, and have a harder time of it until they do. Some stay on the scene, in visible difficulties – a conspicuous presence around town, and known to the authorities – for months at a time, homeless again and again. But only for so long, not for ever. This is a lifestyle and lived circumstance – young, homeless, unsettled, in difficulties and making trouble – that catches up with you in the end, in more ways than one.

Lime Street and Marlborough Hill are much the same from one year to the next.[8] The hostel is always busy, almost always full; there is a continual flux of young people switching between rented bedsit rooms in the same few houses of multiple occupancy on the same few streets, some of them doubling up with friends, stringing together stop-gap measures for a few weeks at a time in the absence of any secure accommodation of

7. Sooner or later, as Richie puts it, 'they'll throw the book at you' (see page 124).
8. In the year to March 2002 over 300 referrals were taken at the Lime Street hostel; of those, 124 young people were actually accommodated.

their own. In any given month, one or other of these properties will be a centre of activity, the place to be; full of noise and smoke and hangers-on, day and night. Every afternoon young people with nothing (better) to do make their way from Stanley Street and Lime Street into Southerton's town centre to get together in twos and threes and mess about and make trouble. Someone or other is always in a mess over something, caught up in some new difficulty or drama, running back and forth between the social services department and the DSS trying to put things right. None of this ever really changes. But the cast of characters does. The names of current residents, printed in marker pen on the whiteboard in the staff office – Tara White (Room 1), Cherie Gibbons (Room 1), Andy Harris (Room 2), Roy Maguire (Room 2), Mark Green (Room 3) ... Daniel Thompson (Room 4) – are never the same from one month to the next. And the same goes for the occupancy of Number 10 Victoria Road or any of the properties on Marlborough Hill: it turns over. The bedsits – the cheapest, shoddy rooms at the very bottom end of Southerton's private rented housing market – are not full to bursting with more and more young people leaving home or Lime Street each week and looking for a place to stay. Rather than an ever-widening circle of more and more young people moving around and around the same few properties, there is a rolling wave – a surge of young people in the same conspicuous difficulties at any one time, temporarily.

Youth is an expansive moment, one in which young people go public with their lives, in all sorts of ways. This is just what the young people passing through the Lime Street hostel do; they hit the streets. And for a while at least, they present a moving target: making society, some small fleck of it, together and on the move, in and between bedsit rooms and emergency accommodation, as friends; all the while restless and unsettled and unwilling.[9] But

9. Restlessness is the key to so much of this; an anxious determination that none of this is for keeps. There is a tenant – a middle-aged, single man – who lives in a bedsit room on Catherine Street, upstairs from where Tara stayed for a few weeks (and Matt after her); he has lived there for as long as anyone can remember – for years; he hardly ever goes out, other than once every two weeks to cash his giro. He keeps a locked cupboard in the shared kitchen downstairs, full of tins of budget foods and bottles of cider (as Matt found out when he forced the lock out of curiosity). It smells in the corridor outside his room. This is not what Tara or any of the others want from the bedsits.

they do so only for so long. After separation and margin – and the elbow-room that comes with liminal status – comes aggregation (see Turner, 1969: 94); and it does come, whether or not the terms of incorporation are all that favourable. Whether or not things sort themselves out or ease off, there comes a point past which life on Springfield Avenue, 'the bedsits and ... drugs and stuff', just doesn't work quite the way it once did.

At which point, if not long before, the young homeless (most of them, almost all of them) *settle* somewhere and slow down: perhaps back at home and making more considered plans; perhaps pregnant and moving to council housing of their own; maybe on probation – the courts having lost patience – and now keeping clear of trouble; or enrolled on a training scheme, having stopped at one address long enough for the Careers Service to pin them down. Still struggling with housing and money worries more than likely, and may be so for years to come, but doing so just shy of coming publicly unstuck. Whichever way, something is over and now behind them. Like Melanie they are still around, but not *around* any more; no longer at large. Not like when they were young and new to all this and had nothing.

Bibliography

Agar, M.H. 1996. *The Professional Stranger (Second Edition)*. London: Academic Press.

Amit, V. (ed.) 2000. *Constructing the Field*. London: Routledge.

Bourdieu, P. 1993. *Sociology in Question*. London: Sage Publications.

Bourgois, P. 1995. *In Search of Respect: Selling Crack in El Barrio*. Cambridge: Cambridge University Press.

Buckingham, A. 1996. A statistical update. In *Charles Murray and the Underclass: The Developing Debate* (ed.) R. Lister. London: IEA Health and Welfare Unit.

Bullock, A., O. Stallybrass and S. Trombley. 1988. *The Fontana Dictionary of Modern Thought (Second Edition)*. London: Fontana Press.

Burgess, A. 1972. *A Clockwork Orange*. London: Penguin Books. First published in 1962.

Bynner, J., L. Chisholm and A. Furlong (eds) 1997. *Youth, Citizenship and Social Change in a European Context*. Aldershot: Ashgate.

Byrne, D. 1999. *Social Exclusion*. Buckingham: Open University Press.

Carlen, P. 1996. *Jigsaw: A Political Criminology of Youth Homelessness*. Buckingham: Open University Press.

CHAR. 1994. *Benefits 1994/1995*. London: CHAR.

Child Poverty Action Group. 2002. *Welfare Benefits Handbook*. London: Child Poverty Action Group.

The Children's Society. 1999. *Still Running: Children on the Streets in the UK*. London: The Children's Society.

Clifford, J. and G.E. Marcus (eds) 1986. *Writing Culture*. London: University of California Press.

Coffield, F., C. Borril and S. Marshall. 1986. *Growing Up at the Margins*. Milton Keynes: Open University Press.

Conrad, J. 1995. *Youth/Heart of Darkness/The End of the Tether*. London: Penguin. First published in 1902.

Corrigan, P. 1993. Doing nothing. In *Resistance through Rituals* (eds) S. Hall and T. Jefferson. London: Routledge. First published in 1975.

Cullen, S. and L. Howe. 1991. People, cases and stereotypes: a study of staff practice in a DSS benefit office. *Cambridge Anthropology* 15, 1–26.

Dahrendorf, R. 1992. Footnotes to the discussion. In *Understanding the Underclass* (ed.) D. Smith. London: Policy Studies Institute.

Davies, N. 1998. *Dark Heart: The Shocking Truth about Hidden Britain*. London: Vintage.

Denzin, N.K. 1997. *Interpretive Ethnography: Ethnographic Practices for the 21st Century*. London: Sage.

Didion, J. 1993. *Slouching Towards Bethlehem*. London: Flamingo. First published in 1968.

Douglas, M. 1984. *Purity and Danger*. London: Ark Paperbacks. First published in 1966.

Duneier, M. 2000. *Sidewalk*: Farrar Straus Giroux.

Evans, A. 1996. *'We don't choose to be homeless ...' (Report of the National Inquiry into Preventing Youth Homelessness)*. London: CHAR.

Furlong, A. and F. Cartmel. 1997. *Young People and Social Change*. Buckingham: Open University Press.

Geertz, C. 2000. *Available Light: Anthropological Reflections on Philosophical Topics*. Princeton: Princeton University Press.

Glasser, I. and R. Bridgman. 1999. *Braving the Street*. New York: Berghahn Books.

Greve, J. 1991. *Homelessness in Britain*. Joseph Rowntree Foundation.

Hannerz, U. 1969. *Soulside: Inquiries into Ghetto Culture and Community*. New York: Columbia University Press.

Hannerz, U. 1992. *Cultural Complexity*. New York: Columbia University Press.

Hebdige, D. 1988. *Hiding in the Light*. London: Routledge.

Hecht, T. 1998. *At Home in the Street: Street Children of Northeast Brazil*. Cambridge: Cambridge University Press.

Howe, L. 1985. The 'deserving' and the 'undeserving': practice in an urban, local social security office. *Journal of Social Policy* 14, 49–72.

Howe, L. 1990. Urban anthropology: trends in its development since 1920. *Cambridge Anthropology* 14, 37–66.

Howe, L. 1998. Scrounger, worker, beggarman, cheat: the dynamics of unemployment and the politics of resistance in Belfast. *Journal of the Royal Anthropological Institute* 4, 531–50.

Hutson, S. 1999. Introduction. In *Homelessness: Public Policies and Private Troubles* (eds) S. Hutson and D. Clapham. London: Cassell.

Hutson, S. and R. Jenkins. 1989. *Taking the Strain: Families, Unemployment and the Transition to Adulthood*. Milton Keynes: Open University Press.

Hutson, S. and M. Liddiard. 1994. *Youth Homelessness*. London: Macmillan.

Jackson, A. (ed.) 1987. *Anthropology at Home*. London: Tavistock.

Jenkins, R. 1990. Dimensions of adulthood in Britain: long-term unemployment and mental handicap. In *Anthropology and the Riddle of the Sphinx* (ed.) P. Spencer. London: Routledge.

Jones, G. 1995. *Leaving Home*. Buckingham: Open University Press.

Jones, G. and C. Wallace. 1992. *Youth, Family and Citizenship*. Buckingham: Open University Press.

Kafka, F. 1994. *The Collected Aphorisms*. London: Penguin.

Keesing, R.M. 1981. *Cultural Anthropology: a Contemporary Perspective*. New York: Holt, Rinehart and Winston.

Kuklick, H. 1991. *The Savage Within*. Cambridge: Cambridge University Press.

Leach, E. 1968. *A Runaway World?* London: The British Broadcasting Corporation.

Liddiard, M. 1990. Youth Homelessness and the Transition to Adulthood. MSc Econ. in Methods and Applications of Social Research: University of Wales, Cardiff.

Liebow, E. 1995. *Tell Them Who I Am*. New York: Penguin.

Lipsky, M. 1980. *Street-Level Bureaucracy*. New York: Russel Sage Foundation.

Lister, R. 1996. Introduction: in search of the 'underclass'. In *Charles Murray and the Underclass: The Developing Debate* (ed.) R. Lister. London: IEA Health and Welfare Unit.

London, J. 1998. *The People of the Abyss*. London: Pluto Press. First published in 1903.

MacDonald, R. 1997. Dangerous youth and the dangerous class. In *Youth, the 'Underclass' and Social Exclusion* (ed.) R. MacDonald. London: Routledge.

MacLeod, J. 1995. *Ain't No Makin' It*. Oxford: Westview Press. First published in 1987.

Malinowski, B. 1978. *Argonauts of the Western Pacific*. London: Routledge. First published in 1922.

Morrow, V. and M. Richards. 1996. *Transitions to Adulthood: A Family Matter?* York: YPS for the Joseph Rowntree Foundation.

Murray, C. 1990. *The Emerging British Underclass*. London: Health and Welfare Unit, Institute of Economic Affairs.

Murray, C. 1994. *Underclass: The Crisis Deepens*. London: Health and Welfare Unit, Institute of Economic Affairs.

National Homeless Alliance. 1999. *The Benefit Guide 1999/2000*. London: National Homeless Alliance.

Ortner, S.B. 1995. Resistance and the problem of ethnographic refusal. *Comparative Studies in Society and History* 37, 173–93.

Orwell, G. 2001. *Orwell and the Dispossessed*. London: Penguin.

Pearson, G. 1983. *Hooligan: A History of Respectable Fears*. London: Macmillan.

Roberts, K. 1993. Career trajectories and the mirage of increased social mobility. In *Youth and Inequality* (eds) I. Bates and G. Riseborough. Buckingham: Open University Press.

Scanlon, P. 2001. *First Step or Last Resort? Young People and Hostel Use on Merseyside*. Liverpool: Shelter Merseyside.

Scott, J.C. 1985. *Weapons of the Weak*. New Haven: Yale University Press.

Sims, G.R. 1976. The dark side of life (from *How the Poor Live*, first published in 1883). In *Into Unknown England, 1866–1913: Selections from the Social Explorers* (ed.) P. Keating. Glasgow: Fontana.

Social Exclusion Unit. 2000. *National Strategy for Neighbourhood Renewal. Report of Policy Action Team 12, Young People*. London: The Stationery Office.

Spradley, J.P. 2000. *You Owe Yourself a Drunk*. Prospect Heights: Waveland Press. First published in 1970.

Strathdee, R. 1992. *No Way Back*. London: Centrepoint.

Thornton, R. 1990. *The New Homeless*. London: SHAC.

Turner, V. 1969. *The Ritual Process*. Chicago: Aldine Publishing Company.

Valentine, C.A. 1968. *Culture and Poverty: Critique and Counter Proposals*. Chicago: University of Chicago Press.

Van Gennep, A. 1960. *The Rites of Passage*. Chicago: University of Chicago Press.

Wade, P. 1997. Introduction. In *Cultural Studies will be the Death of Anthropology* (ed.) P. Wade. Manchester: Group for Debates in Anthropological Theory.

Wallace, C. 1987. *For Richer for Poorer*. London: Tavistock.

Willis, P. 1984a. Youth unemployment: thinking the unthinkable. *Youth and Policy* 2, 17–24.

Willis, P. 1984b. Youth unemployment: a new social state. *New Society* 67, 475–7.

Wyn, J. and R. White. 1997. *Rethinking Youth*. London: Sage.

Index